SELECT
world shop interiors

INDEX
world shop interiors

RESTAURANT&DINING

 06 HAKKASAN Restaurant/London

 10 SOY Restaurant/Utrecht

 **16 SCHUTZENBERGER** Restaurant/Strasbourg

 22 J-CUPS Coffee shop/Berlin

 **26 KOROVA** Restaurant/Paris

 **30 808** Restaurant&Nightclub/Berlin

 **34 UBON** Restaurant/London

 **38 UNIVERSUM LOUNGE** Dining bar/Berlin

FOCUS CONCRETE

 80 SUPPER CLUB Nightclub/Amsterdam

 **86 COFFEE COMPANY** Coffee shop/Amsterdam

 **90 NORMADS** Arabian restaurant&Nightclub/Amsterdam

SPECIALITY STORE&SHOP

 **110 B 54 SUN** Sunglasses shop/Berlin

 **114 MOUDJAHIDIN** Boutique/Paris

 **118 GALERIE FÜR SCHMUCK** Fashion shop/Berlin

 **42 PEUGEOT AVENUE** Cafe/Berlin

 46 DE KAS Restaurant/Amsterdam

 50 BOMA Bar/Berlin

 **54 THE GAUCHO GRILL** Restaurant/London

 58 MONTE'S Restaurant/London

 62 BON Restaurant/Paris

 66 ORIENT Restaurant/London

 **70 CHINA HOUSE** Chinese restaurant/London

 **72 PANAMA** Restaurant/Amsterdam

 **74 CLUB GASCON** Restaurant&Pub/London

76 NEAT French restaurant/London

 96 LAUNDRY INDUSTRY Boutique/London

 **100 RITUALS** Cosmetics store/Amsterdam

 **104 BLENDER** Restaurant/Amsterdam

 **106 SPRING** Restaurant/Amsterdam

 **108 AUSTRALIAN** Ice cream shop/Amsterdam

 120 MANGO Boutique/London

 **122 COMPTOIR GASCON** Food shop/London

 **124 JITROIS** Boutique/London

 **125 BOTTENHEIM** Fashion shop/Berlin

 **126 FRESH&WILD** Health food shop/London

 **127 CHRISTA RENIERS** Jewelry store/Brussels

円形テーブルが並ぶ予約席　Reserved Tables

ダイニングとバーカウンターの間仕切り的に設置されたパーティション　Partition

バーカウンターをテーブル席側より見る　Bar Counter

エントランスの通路。向かって左奥にレセプションがある　Passage

HAKKASAN
Restaurant/London

中国的なソファのデコレーション　Decoration of sofa

HAKKASANは地下鉄のトッテナム・コート・ロードから歩いて2〜3分のハンウエー・プレースに、2001年4月にオープンしたニューアジアンスタイルのレストランである。レセプションは地下1階で、照明を内蔵したカウンターがあり、スポット的にハンギングランプが吊られ、照明をバックに胡蝶蘭が置かれ、花を浮かべたベースにはロウソクの火が灯り、香も焚かれアジア的なもてなしの雰囲気を演出している。

790㎡ある店内は、3つのセクションからなる。コリドーから突き当たりは132席あるレストランで、テーブルにはライトが当てられているがムードを重視してか暗い感じだ。格子状の間仕切りの背後には、40人ほどが座れるバーカウンターがある。また、ソファ・テーブルが置かれているラウンジの壁面は内側から照明が当てられ、メーンとなる柱は幻想的でピンク色の妖しい光を放っている。外光が差し込むような設計となっており、実際の時間を認識できる。各テーブルにも極端なスポット照明というこだわりがあるのが特徴。

Hakkasan is a new Asian style restaurant that opened in April 2001 in Hanway Place, which is a two-to-three-minute walk from Tottenham Court Road subway station. The reception area is in the first underground floor. It features an internally illuminated counter. Lamps are hung here and there. One also finds backlighted moth orchids as well as lighted candles placed in vases with floating flowers. The fragrance and flames produce an atmosphere of Asian hospitality.

The 790-square-meters in the restaurant are divided into three sections. A 132-seat section has tables that are illuminated, but the emphasis is on dim lighting. Behind lattice-shaped partitions one finds a counter bar that seats as many as 40 people. Sofas and tables have been placed inside a lounge. The walls are internally illuminated, and the main pillar chimerically casts a dubious, pink light. The area is designed to permit light to shine in from outside, giving customers a sense of the time of day or night. Another feature is an extremely bright spotlight shining on each table.

1st. 入り口。階段で地下1階のレストランへとアプローチされる　Facade
2nd. レセプション　Reception
3rd. 40人が座れるバーカウンター　Bar Counter
4th. エントランス通路の床に施された花とロウソクの演出
　　　The floor of the passage

ダイニング全景　Dining

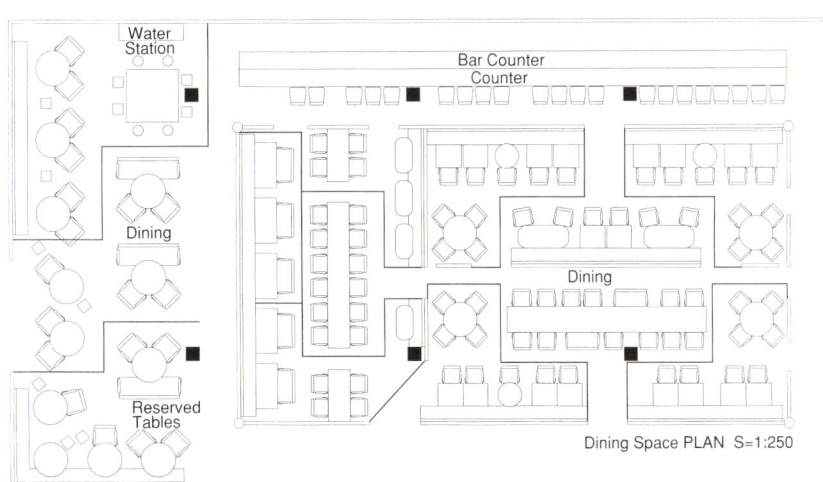

Dining Space PLAN S=1:250

§ HAKKASAN DATA §

Address: 8 Hanway Place London W1 UK　Phone: 020-7927-7000

Architect: Christian Liaigre　Opening date: 2nd. April 2001

Building Area: 790m² 　Seats: Restaurant132 Lounge60 Bar40

Business hours: Lunch12:00〜15:00 (Sat.&Sun.−17:00)

Dinner18:00〜Midnight (Sun.〜23:30)

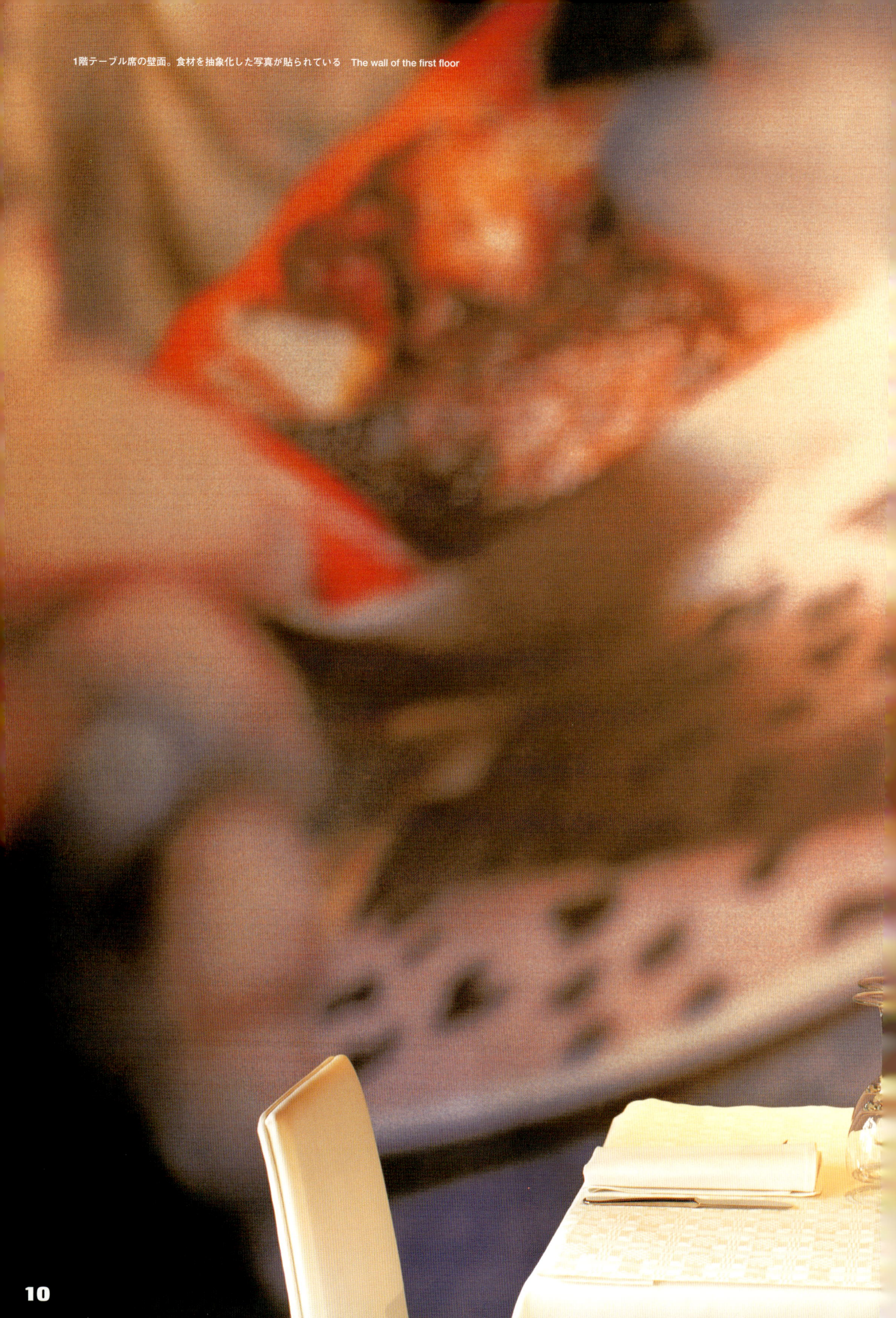

1階テーブル席の壁面。食材を抽象化した写真が貼られている　The wall of the first floor

SOY
Restaurant/Utrecht

オランダ第4の都市・ウトレヒトの運河に面し、小さな店舗が数多く建ち並ぶ旧市街の一角にフレンチ・アジアンスタイルのレストランSOYがオープンし、話題を集めている。ファサードにはシンプルなSOYのロゴがあり、店内は1階、地下1階の2層になっており、コントラストのある構成となっている。

1階には壁面に食材をモチーフにしたかなり抽象的なフルサイズの写真が貼られ、白いテーブルを温かく包み込むかのようである。螺旋階段を下りると、地階のレストランである。こちらの別世界的ダイニングの演出は見事である。昔からある倉庫のアーチを利用した客席は、ブルーの光によってクールな雰囲気に包まれ、壁に皿状に形どられた3個の白いプラスターはエキゾチックなガストロノミーのムードを盛り上げている。

Utrecht is the Netherlands' fourth-largest city. Facing the canal, in a corner of the old town where numerous small shops are located, the French and Asian restaurant Soy is making a name for itself. The facade is decorated with a simple logo bearing the restaurant's name. Soy occupies the first above-ground floor and the first underground floors, and its interior features contrasting elements.

The first-floor walls are decorated with abstract, full-sized photographs that have a cooking-ingredient motif, arranged as if to surround the white tables with warmth. A spiral staircase leads to the eatery's underground section, the admirable design of which gives the impression of dining in another world. The seating, made using an old warehouse arch, is enveloped in a cool ambience of blue light. The white plaster of three dish-shaped objects on the walls creates an exotic, gastronomical mood.

1st.	ファサード	Facade
2nd.	テーブルセッティング	Table
3rd.	1階客席全景	The dining of the first floor
4th.	地階客席への螺旋階段	The spiral staircase to the basement

地階客席から螺旋階段を見る。オレンジとブルーのコントラストがドラマチック　The dining of the basement

螺旋階段側からダイニングを見る　The dining of the basement

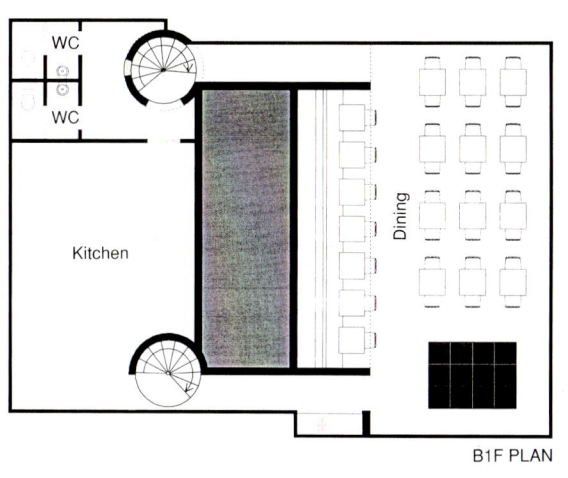

天井の形がかつて倉庫であったことをうかがわせる地下1階客席　A whole view of the dining of the basement

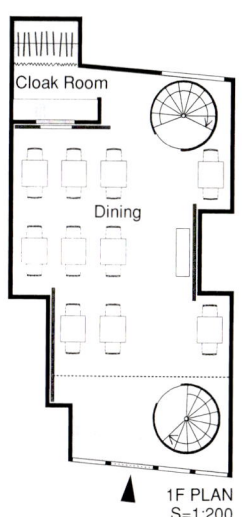

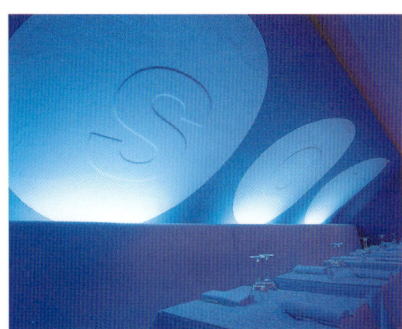

地下1階のソファ席　The dining of the basement

§ SOY DATA §

Address: Twijinstraat15 3511zg. Utrecht Netherlands　Phone: 030-2734431

Architect+Design: Workshop of Wonders　Opening date: 1st. November 2000

Building Area: 200m²　Seats: 56

Business hours: 18:00~ Midnight(Regular Holiday:Monday)

1階のバーカウンターを2階レストランから見る　Bar Counter

窓辺のライトウオール前のイス　Chair in front of the lighting wall

SCHUTZENBERGER
Restaurant/Strasbourg

1st.	ファサード。広場に面して2階のベランダをせり出したデザイン Facade	
2nd.	1階バーのテーブル席 Tables on the first floor	
3rd.	天井のボトルとミラーのハーモニー Ceiling	

1st.	1階バーカウンター前のロングテーブル Big table on the first floor	
2nd.	1階バーカウンターのビアサーバー。ビール会社の経営だけに種類は豊富 Beer server	
3rd.	1階エントランスから見た客席 The dining of the first floor	

2階レストラン　The dining of the second floor

このレストランは、ドイツと国境を接するストラスブールで1860年に創業したビール会社の直営である。現社長であるマリー・ローレン・ムラー氏は、新ミレニアムを記念して建築家ジャン・ヌーベルを起用し、新感覚のブラッスリー・カフェレストランを作り上げた。

レストラン内部へは広場と裏通りの両サイドからアクセスされる。中央には長いバーカウンターがあり、並行してメタリックの長いテーブルが置かれ、背後にはきらめくようなガラスのスクリーンがある。バーの後部から緩やかなスロープがあり、2階のレストランへアプローチしている。

天井のアトリウム空間には、1932年に建設されたというビールビンの底をモザイクのようにデザインした屋根があり、呼応するようにミラーを設置し、輝きの相乗効果を狙っている。空間全体にガラス、メタル、ミラーといったクールな素材を多用し、光と交差させて、洗練された都会的な温かさをクリエートしている。

This restaurant is directly managed by a beer company established in 1860 in Strasbourg, a city on the border with Germany. Marie Lorraine Muller, the current company president, hired architect Jean Nouvel to build this new type of brasserie/cafe restaurant to commemorate the new millenium.

Schutzenberger can be entered from either side, both from a plaza and from a back street. In the center of the interior is a long bar counter, parallel with which has been placed a long, metallic table. Behind this table is a flickering glass screen. A gentle slope rises from the rear of the bar to the second-floor restaurant.

The atrium space near the ceiling features a roof designed and built in 1932 as a kind of mosaic made from beer bottles. By installing mirrors that reflect one another, the designer was aiming for a radiance-multiplying effect. The overall space makes use of cool materials such as glass, metal and mirrors to produce crisscrossing light and create a refined, urban warmth.

2階ベランダ　Veranda

オードブルの例　Hors d'oeuvre

テーブル席のカラーコーディネート　Detail of the table

1階と2階をつなぐ長いスロープ　Slope to the second floor

§ SCHUTZENBERGER DATA §

Address: 29-31 Rue des Grandes Arcades 6700 Strasbourg France

Architect+Design: Jean Nouvel

Opening date: 22nd. November 1999

Building Area: 1000m^2　Seats: 300

Average Price for lunch: 100francs　Average Price for dinner: 120francs

湾曲した5枚のパネルは光の色の変化により店内のムードを演出する　Lighting wall

J-CUPS
Coffee shop/Berlin

J-CUPSは55㎡とコンパクトながら、立ち飲みスタイルでコーヒーを提供する未来感覚のカフェである。経営者であるヤコブス・カフェは、20年の歴史を持ち、ドイツでもよく知られたブランドである。近年、ドイツでは若者のコーヒー離れが顕著であり、その若者たちにコーヒーに再び目を向けてもらおうと出店された。ソフトドリンクを飲むような雰囲気と手軽さをテーマとし、16歳から26歳をターゲットに、試行錯誤を繰り返しコンセプトを構築した。

店内はクール、かつシンプルを基調に、サイン、ロゴ、インテリアがまとめられ、壁面にはタッチコントロール式のパネルを設置して、光の変化を若者にアピールしている。

同じコンセプトのショップが市内にもう1軒あり、今後はデュッセルドルフ、ケルンといった都市にも出店計画があるという。また、ショッピングセンター、映画館、主要駅にも出店される予定である。

With only 55 square meters, the futuristic cafe J-Cups is a compact establishment where customers drink their coffee standing up. Jacobs Cafe, which manages J-Cups, has a 20-year history and is a well-known brand in Germany. In recent years, young people in Germany have been remarkably aloof toward coffee, and this cafe was opened to acquaint them with the beverage's excellent taste. The cafe, which was designed to have the kind of informal atmosphere in which one would drink a soft drink, targets 16- to 26-year-olds, and was built with the concept of trial and error in mind.

Inside, the restaurant brings together a sign, a logo and other interior design elements in a harmony of coolness and simplicity. A touch-control-style panel with changing lights was installed on the wall to appeal to young people.

There is one other cafe with the same concept in Berlin, and there are plans to open shops in the cities of Düsseldorf and Köln as well, and also in shopping centers, movie theaters and major train stations.

1st.　シンプルなデザインのレジカウンター　Cash register
2nd.　プラスチックとメタルからなる立ち飲みカウンター　Counter

§ J-CUPS DATA §

Address: Unter den Linden 80 Berlin Germany　Phone:030-2838-7750
Interior designer: Jörg Philipp/Yellowpeople Kommunikation　Opening date: October 2000
Building Area:55m²

ファサード。夏の間はオープンテラスとなる　Facade

暖色のカラーでコーディネートされた、最奥の客席わきに設けられた個室的雰囲気のテーブル席　A view of the dining table

KOROVA
Restaurant/Paris

パリ8区のシャンゼリゼ大通りに通ずるマルベウフ通りに、新感覚のフランスレストランKOROVAがオープンした。KOROVAとはロシア語で「牛」を意味し、2000年10月に開店した。

白いテーブル、レザー貼りの低いテーブル、奥の部屋の中央には円形のアクアリュームと、インテリアは白とベージュを基調とし、天井にはオレンジ色の照明を配して空間のバランスを取っている。また、静かな雰囲気の中にプラスチック等、1970年代のデザイン感覚をイメージさせるものが多い。

中央にあるバーでは35種類以上のシャンパンやカクテルが供され、10ブランド以上の、他のレストランでは手に入らないミネラルウオーターも用意されている。平均客単価はランチが350フラン、ディナーが500フランとやや高めであるが、それだけの価値は見いだせそうである。

The new-style French restaurant Korova is located on Paris' Rue Marbeuf, which connects with Avenue des Champs Elysées, located in the 8th District. Korova, which means cow in Russian, opened in October 2000.

The restaurant contains both white tables and low, leather-covered tables. There is a round acquarium in the back room. The interior achieves a harmony of white and beige, with the ceiling and its orange light fixtures balancing the space. Amid this quiet atmosphere one finds several items, some plastic, that recall the design of the 1970s.

A bar in the center offers more than 35 types of champagne and cocktails, along with more than 10 brands of mineral water that are unavailable at other restaurants. The average dining cost, at 350 francs for lunch and 500 francs for dinner, is a little on the expensive side, but one gets the impression it is worth it.

1st.　店内中央にあるバーカウンター　Bar counter
2nd.　ミラーで演出されたテーブル席　A view of the dining table
3rd.　道路側の客席　The dining table by the windowside
4th.　最奥の客席に設置された円形のアクアリューム
　　　The round acquarium in the back room

アクアリュームわきのテーブル席
The dining table by the acquarium

エントランス側の客席全景。天井のオレンジ色の照明が、白とベージュを基調とした空間のアクセントとなっている
The dining of the entranceside

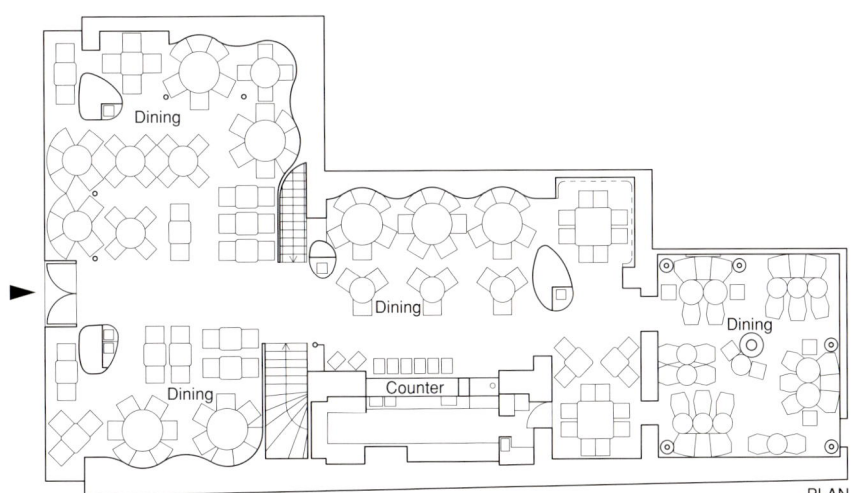

PLAN

§ KOROVA DATA §

Address: 33 Rue Marbeuf 75008 Paris France   Phone: 01-53899393

Interior designer: Christian Biecher   Opening date: 23rd. October 2000   Building Area: 450m^2 Seats:150

Average Price for lunch: 350francs   Average Price for dinner: 500francs   Business hours: 8:00~Midnight

金色の柱とアクアリュームが調和を見せるナイトクラブのコーナー　Nightclub

808
Restaurant&Nightclub/Berlin

1st. 「ウオータージェット」と名付けられたステンレス製のテーブル　Stainless-steel table named "Waterjets"

2nd. この店オリジナルのテーブルとイス　A view of the restaurant

レストラン全景。奥がナイトクラブとなっている　A view of the restaurant

レストランの窓際の客席　The dining table of the restaurant

柱のディテール　Detail of the column

この店舗は、ベルリン・ミット地区のオラニエンバーガー駅の近くにあるナイトクラブ+レストランである。

店内はステンレスのカウンターと、メタリックのウオールペーパーでカバーされた金色の2本のコロンが空間を支配している。エントランスから入った右側には夕方6時からオープンするナイトクラブがあり、同様の円柱が空間を支えている。バーカウンターサイドには大きなアクアリュームがあり、かなりリラックスしたスペースとなっている。テーブルとイスは細いメタルの脚で統一されたデザインである。

レストラン内にはやはり細いメタルの脚の背の高いイス・テーブルセットがあり、窓辺のコーナーには「ウオータージェット」と呼ばれるステンレス製の光るテーブルが置いてある。これらは設計者が独自に開発したもので、新素材のデザイン開発に時間と労力をつぎ込んでいる。

808 is a nightclub and restaurant located near Oranienburger station in the Mitte district of Berlin.

The interior features a stainless-steel counter and two golden columns covered in metallic wallpaper that dominate the space. To the right of the entrance is a nightclub that opens at 6 p.m. It contains another column of the same type. The relaxed space on the bar-counter side of the club contains a large acquarium. The tables and chairs all have the same design, which includes thin metal legs.

Unsurprisingly, the tall chairs and tables in the restaurant also have thin metal legs. Shiny, stainless-steel tables called Waterjets are found by the restaurant's corner windows. Considerable time and trouble were apparently spent on their design.

カウンター全景　Counter

レストラン側のカウンター　Counter　　　　　　　バーカウンターのビアサーバー　Beer server

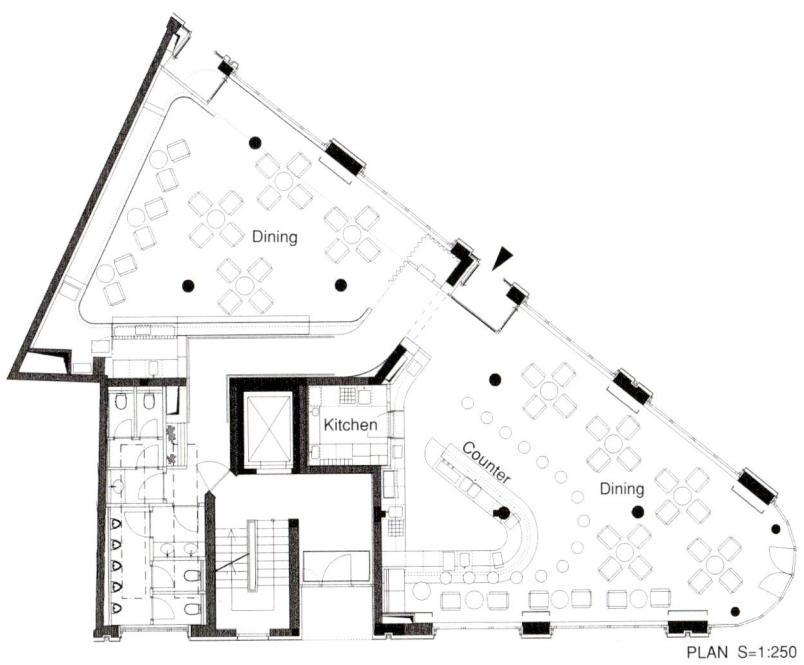

PLAN S=1:250

§ 808 DATA §

Address: Oranienburger Strasse 42-43 Berlin Mitte Germany　Phone: 030-61401350

Interior designer: Player&Franz Studio　Opening date: December 1999

Building Area: 270m²　Seats:160

1st. UBONはこのブルーのビルの最上階にある
UBON is on the top of the building

2nd. 窓際のテーブル席　Dining table besides the window

レセプション　Reception

UBON
Restaurant/London

UBONの入り口まわり。右手がレセプション　Entrance

スシバー。中央がシェフの中村氏　Sushi bar

カウンター席　Counter

琥珀のスダレ状のスクリーンのディテール　Detail of the screen

テームズ川を一望できるテーブル席　Dining table

客席全景　A whole view of the dining

高価ながらもヘルシーブームも手伝って、ヨーロッパの各都市では日本食が定着しつつある。ニューヨークで俳優のロバート・デ・ニーロが仕掛けたNOBUが大ヒットし、東京、ミラノでも出店された。ロンドンではメトロポリタンホテル内の店舗に続いて2店めで、キャナリー・ワーフのウエストフェリー・サーカスのビルの最上階にある。

UBONとはNOBUを単に逆さ読みしたものである。総ガラス張りの店内は、テームズ川の眺望もメニューの一部であるかのようで、その付加価値は抜群である。エントランスサイドにはシェフの中村氏が職人技を披露するスシバーがある。窓には琥珀のスダレ状のスクリーンが垂れ下がり、外光を浴びて独特な光を放っている。店内から見る晴れた日の日没は筆舌に尽くし難く、そういう日は予約がなかなか取れないとのことである。

Japanese food continues to establish itself in European cities as an expensive but healthy culinary option. Actor Robert De Niro's hit New York restaurant Nobu has already opened outlets in Tokyo and Milano. Ubon, located on the top of a building in Westferry Circus, Canary Wharf, is the second location in London, having opened after an outlet in the Metropolitan Hotel.

The name Ubon is simply Nobu spelled backwards. The glass-windowed interior provides a view of the Thames River that is delicious enough to be a menu item and adds exceptional value to the dining experience. On the entrance side is a sushi bar that puts Chef Nakamura's craftsmanship on full display. Amber bamboo screens hang in the windows, where they filter the light from outside to create a peculiar effect. The view of a sunset from inside Ubon is beyond description, and on days when a spectacular sunset is expected, it is hard to get a reservation.

§ UBON DATA §

Address: 34 Westferry Circus Canary Wharf London E14 8RR UK　Phone: 020-77197800
Interior designer: United Designers　Building Area: 195m²　Seats: 125
Business hours: Lunch12:00~14:30(Mon.~Fri.)　Dinner18:00~22:15(Mon.~Sat.)

ラウンジ　A view of the lounge

メニューをスマートに収納できるテーブルのアイデア　Detail of the round table

月面と地球の写真がムードを醸し出す
The wall of the lounge

UNIVERSUM LOUNGE
Dining bar/Berlin

夜になるとラウンジが月の軌道を漂っているかのような錯覚に陥る　The wall of the lounge at night

この店はかつては劇場で現在は映画館となっているUniversumに隣接している　Facade

夜の外部客席　Outdoor section

カウンターの腰とイス　Counter and chair

市民から「クーダム」という名称で親しまれているKur Fürstendamm通りにあるこの店は、1930年代にはベルリン最大の映画館として、80年代にはコンテンポラリーの劇場として有名であったが、通りの反対側でイタリアレストランを経営するフランコ・フランクッチ氏が2001年1月15日にオープンさせたものである。

インテリアは60年代のアポロの月面着陸をイメージしたもので、壁面には当時世界の人々の注目を集めた写真の数々が飾ってあり、白く長いソファはアポロのインテリアからヒントを得た。無重力でも飛ばされないように、しっかりと固定されている。バーに置いてある低いラウンドテーブルにはメニューを立てるためのスリットがあり、スマートなデザインである。

開演前後のシャンパンとカクテルの歓談の場として好評を得、夏季には広いスペースを利用した野外のグリルとドリンク、ビールでにぎわいを見せ、夜更けまで楽しそうな笑い声が絶えない。

This restaurant on Kur Fürstendamm, a street Berliners warmly refer to by the nickname Kurdamm, was famous in the 1930s as the largest movie theater in city, and in the 80s as a contemporary live theater. Franco Francucci, who manages an Italian restaurant across the street, opened Universum Lounge on Jan. 15, 2001.

The interior is based on the theme of the Apollo 11 spacecraft's moon landing in the 1960s. The walls are decorated with photographs documenting people's excitement at the event, and the long, white sofa was designed taking cues from the interior of Apollo 11. It is firmly affixed to the floor so as not to float away in zero gravity. The smartly designed, low, round tables in the bar have slits to hold menus.

Universum Lounge is known as a place to gather for champagne, cocktails and pleasant conversation before and after a theatrical opening. During the summer, its large outdoor section is crowded with customers who come for grilled food, drinks and beer, and customers can be heard laughing until late at night.

カウンター　Counter

ソファのデザインはアポロ宇宙船のインテリアにヒントを得た　Sofa　　　　ブロンズをランダムに組み合わせたカウンターの腰　Detail of the counter

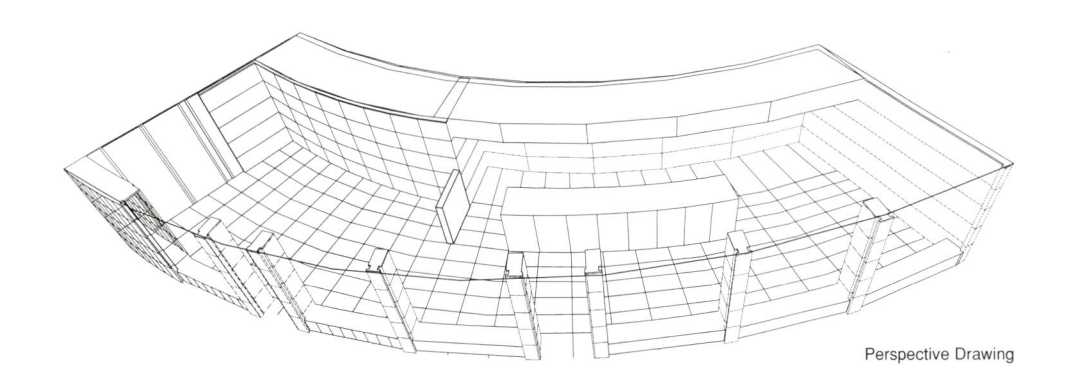

Perspective Drawing

§ UNIVERSUM LOUNGE DATA §

Address: Kurfürstendamm 153 10709 Berlin Germany　Owner: Franco Francucci
Interior designer: Player&Franz Studio　Opening date: 15th. January 2001
Building Area: 81m²　Seats:82

ショールーム前のカフェ　Facade

赤で統一された2階の廊下。赤一色であるが、不思議と落ち着きを感じさせる空間に仕上がっている　Passage of the second floor

PEUGEOT AVENUE
Cafe/Berlin

入り口まわり　Entrance

バーコーナーのカウンター　Bar counter

2階階段わきから見る　Passage of the second floor

フランスの自動車メーカー、プジョー社が誇るショールーム兼カフェである。2001年3月、ベルリンのウンター・デン・リンデンにオープンした。ガラスのファサードは高さ6㎡におよび、2階建てで面積は900㎡の規模である。

ショールームに足を踏み入れると、2階にはカフェ・ド・フランスがあり、ショールーム奥から階段でアプローチされる。中央にバーカウンターがあり、赤いコリドーがカフェとなっている。レストラン席はバンケットに囲まれ、壁にはプジョーの車の歴史を綴った写真が飾ってあり、赤いジュータン、白いテーブル、ロウソクのブルーのガラス器は洗練されたパリの雰囲気を演出している。

このプジョー・アベニューは、プジョー社の世界に先駆けた最初のイメージプロジェクトで、21世紀に向けたさわやかなスピリットが感じられる。

Combined cafe and showroom Peugeot Avenue is the pride of the French automaker. It opened in Berlin's Unter den Linden in March 2001. Peugeot Avenue has a 6-meter-high glass facade, two stories and 900 square meters of floor space.

Stepping into the showroom, the visitor can see Café de France on the second floor. The cafe is reached via a staircase inside. In the center is a bar counter, and a red corridor serves as the actual cafe. Surrounding the restaurant seating is a banquet room whose walls are decorated with photographs depicting the history of Peugeot automobiles. The red carpet, white tables, and blue glass candleholders reproduce the refined atmosphere of Paris.

Peugeot Avenue, Peugeot's first major project to polish its public image, communicates the refreshing spirit of the 21st. century.

2階バーコーナー　Bar of the second floor

レストランのテーブルセッティング　Dining table of the restaurant

レストラン全景　Restaurant of the second floor

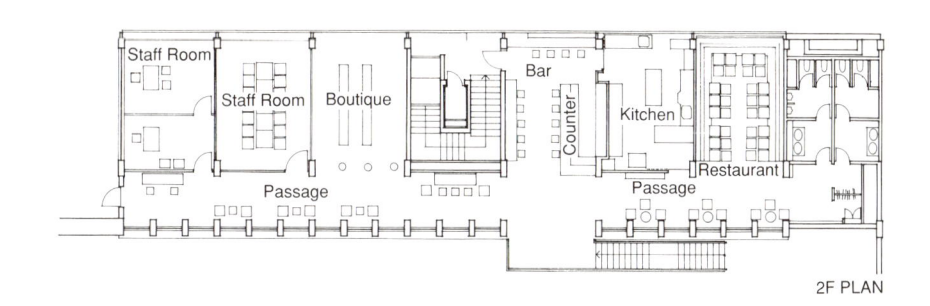

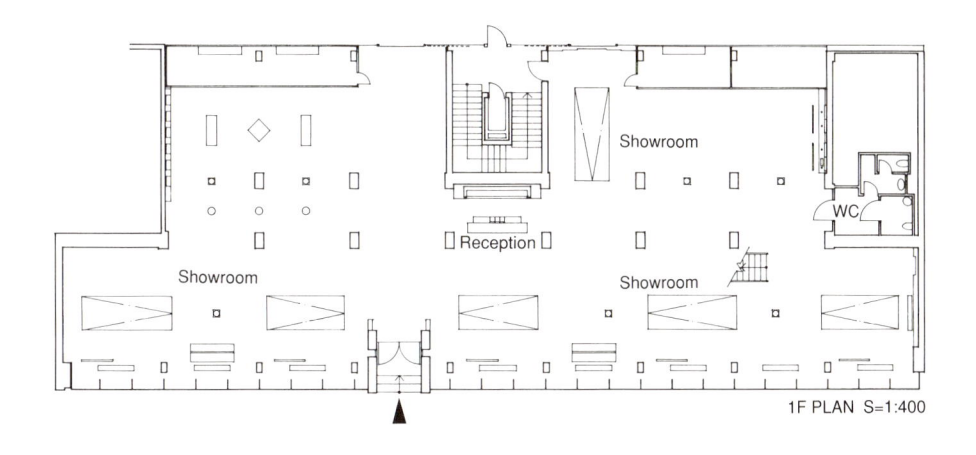

2F PLAN

1F PLAN S=1:400

§ PEUGEOT AVENUE DATA §

Address: Unter den Linden 62-68 D-10117 Berlin Germany   Phone: 030-3022605101

Architect: Sagvez and Partners   Design: Yves Taralon

Opening date: 30th. March 2001   Building Area:900m²   Seats(Cafe): 60

建物全景。既存の温室を飲食空間に改装した　Facade

メーンダイニング全景。天井には新たに空調設備が付け加えられた　A whole view of the main dining

DE KAS
Restaurant/Amsterdam

1st.	レストランに隣接するハーブ園 Herb garden next door to the restaurant
2nd.	テーブルとイス　Dining table and chair
3rd.	レストランができるまでを紹介した写真の数々 Photos for construction of the restaurant

1st.	ユニークな業態の発案者である、オーナーのゲアート・ヤン・ハーグマン氏 Mr.Gert Jan Hageman, the owner
2nd.	エントランス側より見る　A view of the dining from the entrance
3rd.	レストラン奥にあるバーカウンター　Bar counter

入り口まわり　Entrance

窓際のテーブル席　Dining table besides the window

「温室とナーサリー（菜園）をレストランに」……オーナーシェフのゲアート・ヤン・ハーグマン氏の4年を費やしたプロジェクトが実を結び、このレストランは2001年1月にオープンした。グルメのアムステルダム市民やレストラン関係者の関心を集めている。

古くからあった温室の改造は建築家のピエット・ブーンが手掛け、構造には手をつけずにベンチレーションシステムの設置、断熱ガラスに入れ替えといった具合に改装が行われ、窓辺にはオリーブを植え、チーク材のテーブルやモダン家具を配し、1000㎡、170席の快適なレストランへと生まれ変わった。

無農薬野菜を隣接するナーサリーで栽培し、そのまま食材に使うため、ヘルシー志向や温室そのものがレストランになったという珍しい発想が受け、連日冷蔵庫には食材がなくなってしまうほどだという。当然セットメニューも頻繁に変えなくてはならない。旅行エージェントからの問い合わせも多く、第2号店を出店する可能性も出てきている。

A four-year project by owner/chef Gert Jan Hageman bore fruit when the restaurant De Kas opened in January 2001. De Kas is earning the admiration of Amsterdam's gourmand residents and restaurant-industry insiders.

Architect Piet Boon remodeled an old greenhouse to create this comfortable restaurant with 1,000 square meters of floor space and 170 seats. Without changing the building's structure, he installed a ventilation system and substituted in insulated glass, then planted olive trees near the windows and arranged teak tables and modern furniture.

De Kas grows organic vegetables in its nursery and uses them in its dishes, actualizing the unusual concept of a healthful restaurant in a greenhouse. The refrigerator is emptied daily and the set menu is changed frequently. De Kas gets a lot of inquiries from travel agents, and the owner says a second location is a possibility.

§ DE KAS DATA §

Address: Kamerlingh Onneslaan 3. 1097 DE Amsterdam Netherlands　Phone: 020-4624562
Owner: Gert Jan Hageman　Architect+Design: Piet Boon
Opening date: 15th. January 2001　Building Area: 1000m^2　Seats: 170
Average Price for lunch: 90guilders　Average Price for dinner: 140guilders

入り口を入って右側の、円形テーブルが並ぶ客席を見る　A view of the rightward dining

壁面に大胆にアート作品をあしらった反対側の客席　　A view of the leftward dining

BOMA
Bar/Berlin

51

1st.	入り口。入り口を入ると客席は左右に分かれている	Entrance
2nd.	アート作品が飾られた側の客席から見る	Dining
3rd.	壁面のカウンターには赤い照明が妖しく光る	Counter

1st.	ペパーを形どった真っ赤な照明器具はオーナーのデザイン	Dining
2nd.	1980年代をイメージしたカウンターバックの照明	Lighting fixture

バーカウンター　Bar counter

BOMAとは聞き慣れない名前であるが、オーナーのマルコポーロ・ヴェニース氏によればBar of Modern Artの頭文字であるそうだ。ベルリンのナイトスポットとして人気を集めており、夜9時を過ぎるとエントランス付近に仮設のDJブースが設置され、大いに活気づく。

マルコポーロ氏自身がアーチストであり、市内でほかにバーを2軒経営している。ここは3軒めの店である。同氏は1985年にギリシャから移住してきたが、当時のヨーロッパのインテリアデザインの印象が壁面にあしらってあり、モダンアートとフュージョンさせて独自の雰囲気を作り出している。サラダ、パスタ、ピザに加えフォンデューも人気があり、カクテルは250種類のバリエーションを用意している。中でもコーヒーカクテルは独自のアイデアだという。

夜になると照明が極端に落とされ、ロウソク、天井のスリットからの照明、バーカウンターの下のボックス照明、ペパーを形どった真っ赤なオブジェ照明などが主役となる。

Boma is a name that is hard to get used to, but owner Markopoulos Vannis says it is an acronym for Bar of Modern Art. Boma is gaining popularity as a Berlin nightspot; after 9 p.m., when a DJ booth is set up near the entrance, the place really gets going.

Mr. Vannis is himself an artist, and he manages two other bars in the city. He immigrated to Germany from Greece in 1985. At the time his impression of European interior design was one of decorated walls. He fused this image with modern art to create an original atmosphere. Popular foods include salad, pasta, pizza and fondue, and there are over 250 varieties of cocktail, including an original coffee cocktail.

At night the lights are turned down low, and candles, ceiling slits that let in light, box lights under the bar and deep red, pepper objets d'art take center stage.

§ BOMA DATA §

Address: Neue Schonhauser Str. 10 10178 Berlin Germany   Phone: 030-27594955
Owner: Markopoulos Vannis   Interior designer: Markopoulos Vannis
Opening date: October 2000   Building Area: 140m²
Business hours: 10:00~Midnight

奥から見た客席　Dining area

THE GAUCHO GRILL
Restaurant/London

オランダが本社のTHE GAUCHO GRILLは、ロンドン、グラスゴー、マンチェスター等、全英7カ所で展開している。チェルシー地区のスローンアベニューのこの店は最新のものである。アルゼンチンビーフをはじめバラエティーに富んだ肉料理、シーフード、ベジタリアン用のメニューがあり、アルゼンチンワインと6㎡あるバーカウンターで供されるカクテルには定評がある。

窓辺の客席の柱はメッシュ状のメタルで覆われ、イスはメタルと革、木製の脚に座は革張りといったラテンアメリカ特有のデザインとなっている。エントランス奥は段差のあるスプリットレベルとなっていて、20～60人用のビュッフェシートがあり、パーティー用スペースとして使用されている。昼間のランチタイムはビジネスマンに、夜は地元チェルシー在住の顧客でにぎわい、本格的ビーフ料理を嗜好する人たちに好評を得ている。

The Gaucho Grill, a restaurant chain headquartered in the Netherlands, has seven locations in England, including outlets in London, Glasgow and Manchester. This outlet on Sloane Avenue in the Chelsea district is the newest. The menu features a rich variety of meat dishes, which start with Argentine beef, and it also includes seafood and vegetarian dishes. The cocktails served at the bar, which include six varieties of Argentine wine, have a well-established reputation.

The pillars in the seating area near the window are covered with mesh-type metal, and the chairs are composed of metal, leather and wood. With the leather stretched across wooden legs, their design is distinctly Latin American. Beyond the entrance is a split-level area containing buffet seating for between 20 and 60 people. This space is used for parties. This Gaucho Grill outlet bustles with businessmen at lunchtime and with Chelsea residents at night, and it enjoys a good reputation among fans of authentic beef dishes.

1st.　入り口　Entrance
2nd.　レセプション　Reception
3rd.　テーブルセッティング　Dining table

§ THE GAUCHO GRILL DATA §

Address: 89 Sloane Avenue London SW3 UK　Phone: 020-584-9901
Interior designer: Gioma Restaurants Plc.
Opening date: November 2000　Seats: 126
Average Price for lunch: 15pounds
Average Price for dinner: 27pounds
Business hours: Lunch12:00～17:00　Dinner18:00～23:00

客席奥から見る　Dining area

中央にあるバーカウンター　Bar counter

レセプションラウンジ　Reception lounge

クラブのシャンパン＆シガーショップ　Champagne and cigar shop

MONTE'S
Restaurant/London

入り口　Facade

レセプション　Reception

テーブルセッティング　Dining table

円形の天井照明のディテール　Detail of the ceiling

バーカウンターと円形天井　Bar counter and round ceiling

ラウンジ（レストラン）　Lounge(Restaurant)

この店は、ロンドンのナイトブリッジのスローンストリートに2000年8月にオープンした。2001年5月にはバーが新装オープンした。通りに面したシガーショップと入り口を別にしたフレンチレストラン風のファサードはよく目立つ。ロンドンでも最もファッショナブルなエリアだけに、レセプションラウンジのピンク色のソファやクッションなどは、スポットライトを浴び華麗な雰囲気を醸し出している。

バーの中央にはゴールド色のスタッコ風にペイントされた円形のシーリングがあり、周囲にはプラスターとガラスの小片に照明を内蔵させた彫刻的なリングがあしらわれ、クラブメンバーズの輪を象徴しているかのようである。また、天井のパンチングされたメタルの照明器具は、トルキッシュブルーの鮮やかな光を放っている。

このレストランでは、平日の昼12時から2時15分までメンバー以外にもランチを提供しており、ビジネスマン等に好評である。

Monte's opened on Sloane Street in Knightbridge, London, in August 2000. In May 2001, its bar was remodeled. Monte's has an eye-catching French restaurantlike facade facing the street. As befits its location in the most fashionable part of London, the eatery's reception lounge, with its spotlighted pink sofa and cushions, brings about a splendid atmosphere.

In the center of the Monte's bar is a rounded ceiling colored with a golden, stucco-type paint. Sculpturelike rings, arranged to surround this ceiling, seem to symbolize the figurative circles of the club members. Punched metal light fixtures on the ceiling cast a brilliant, Turkish blue light.

Monte's serves lunch to nonmembers from noon to 2:15, and enjoys a favorable reputation among businesspeople.

§ MONTE'S DATA §

Address: 164 Sloane Street London SW1 UK   Phone :020-72450896
Interior designer: Wentworth Design   Opening date:Bar May 2001 Restaurant August 2000   Seats: Total120
Average Price for lunch: 23pounds   Average Price for dinner: 35pounds
Business hours: Lunch12:00~14:15   Dinner18:00~(Members only)

モニターが設置された最奥の客席　Dining area

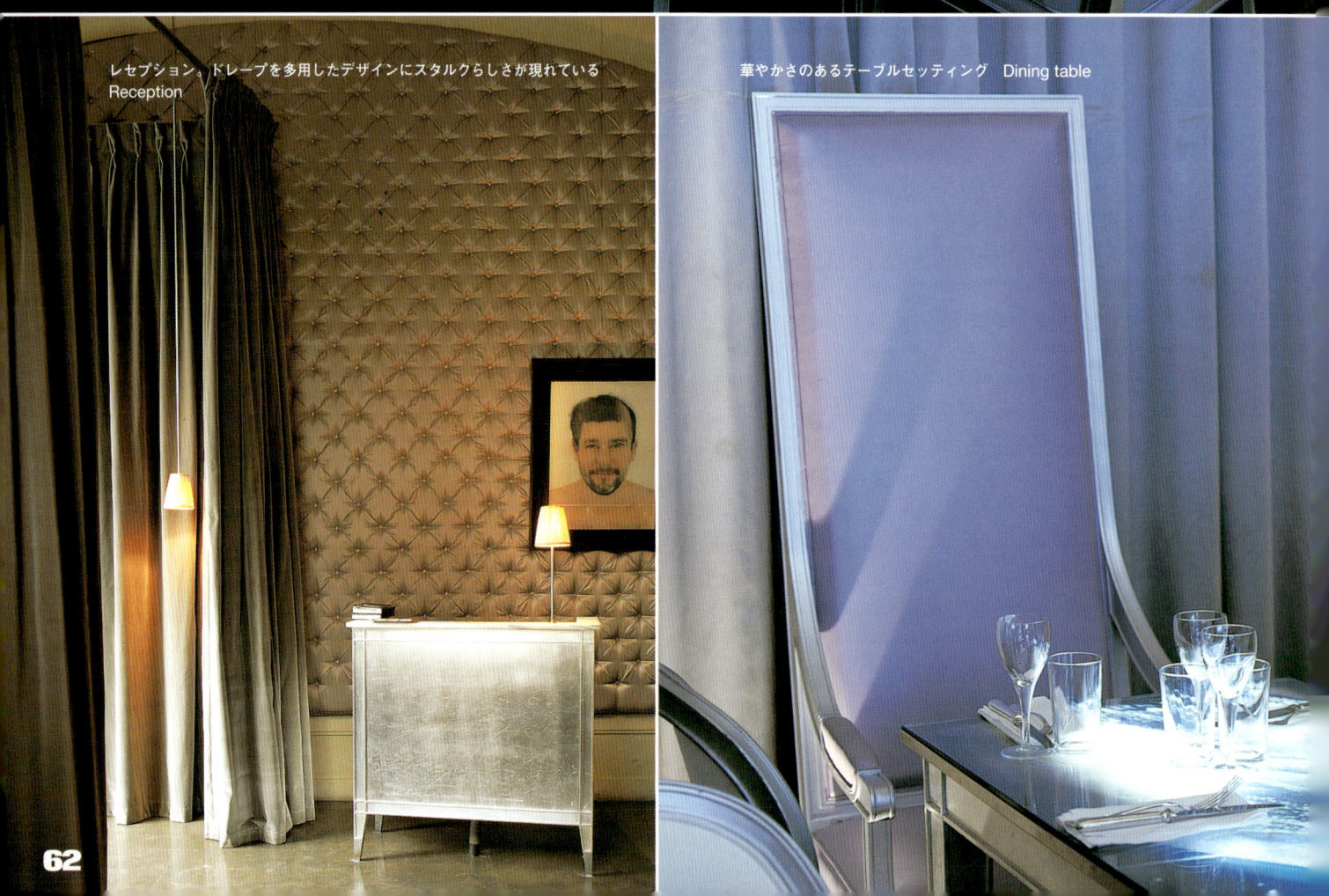

レセプション。ドレープを多用したデザインにスタルクらしさが現れている
Reception

華やかさのあるテーブルセッティング　Dining table

スシバー。日本の回転寿司の機構を組み入れている　Sushi bar

BON
Restaurant/Paris

テーブルセッティング　Table setting

スシバーのテーブルセッティング　Sushi bar　　通路に設置されたワインセラー　Wine cellar

テーブルセッティング　Table setting

ミラーによる演出がなされたテーブル席　Dining table　　　　　　　　　　　トイレ　Restroom

BONはパリの高級住宅地として有名な16区のポンペ通りにある。経営はLaurent Taieb、Alain Attal、それにPhilippe Starckが協同でオープンさせた。インテリアはStarck自ら手掛けている。

このレストランの前身は、1980年代の半ばに注目を集めたOLEVEというレストランである。今回のリニューアルに際し、顧客のさまざまなニーズに対応できるように、スシバー、バーカウンターをはじめ、コリドーの両側にはStarckブランドのワインや小物、フード類のショップを配し、奥のレストランには4カ所の食空間を創作している。

各スペースにはドレープを使用し、トイレまでこだわったデザインであるところにStarckらしさが感じられる。全体的には広く親しみやすい雰囲気で、高級レストランが持つ重苦しさがないのが特徴と言える。

Bon is located on Rue de la Pompe, a famous, high-class residential street in Paris' 16th district. The restaurant was opened and is managed by Laurent Taieb, Alain Attal and Philippe Starck. Starck designed the interior himself.

Bon's predecessor was a restaurant called Oleve that was well-known in the mid-1980s. In the process of creating Bon, Starck renewed the space to meet diverse customer needs. He created a sushi bar; a bar counter; a shop that sells Starck-brand wine, accessories and foods and takes up space on each side of the corridor; and a main restaurant in the back comprising four dining areas.

With drapes used in each part of Bon and attention to design apparent even in the restrooms, Starck's touch is palpable. The overall aura is one of spaciousness and warmth, and the oppressiveness often found in upscale restaurants is noticeably absent.

§ BON DATA §

Address: 25 Rue de la Pompe 75016 Paris France   Phone: 01-40727000
Interior designer: Philippe Starck+Dorothee Boissier   Opening date: October 2000
Business hours: Lunch12:00~15:00   Restaurant20:00~0:30   Salon:15:00~19:00

バーラウンジ全景　Bar lounge

クリッパーバー。1930年代、アメリカ・中国間を飛んだ飛行機の翼をイメージしたデザイン　Clipper Bar

ORIENT
Restaurant/London

レセプション。壁面には1930年代の中国の写真が飾られている　Reception

バーカウンターわきのラウンジ　Lounge

抽象画が飾られているレストランのソファ席　Dining Table

最奥のVIPルーム　Private dining room

1階エントランス・アプローチ。エレベーターもしくは階段で2階へと導かれる　Entrance

このレストランは、入り口は別であるが、CHINA HOUSE（70ページ）と同じ建物の2階で営業している。1階エントランスの右側にはネオンサインを浮き彫りにしたかのようなグラフィカルなモダンアートが掛けられており、エレベーターによって2階へとアプローチされる。

ピカデリー（通りの名称）に面してクリッパーバーがある。これは1930年代、アメリカ・中国間を飛んだ飛行機をイメージしたバーで、カウンターにはレザーとアルミを使用したイスが並び、背後には格納庫をイメージした壁と天井がある。レストランのインテリアにはモダンアートや抽象画を多く配し、中でもこの歴史的建造物がハスの花で囲まれている絵は、ラウンドテーブルと見事な調和を見せている。

奥には18人が座れるプライベートのダイニングルームがあり、少人数のパーティーには格好のスペースとなっており、落ち着きのある豪華さが感じられる。厨房はCHINA HOUSEと共用とのことだが、グレードアップしたオリエンタル風のメニューが楽しめる。

This restaurant is in on the second floor of the building that houses China House(page70), but it has a separate entrance. To the right of the first floor entrance hangs graphical modern art that looks like a neon sign might if it were somehow transformed into an embossed carving. An elevator takes patrons to the second floor.

A bar called the Clipper Bar faces Piccadilly street. It was designed in the image of an airplane that flew between the United States and China in the 1930s. The counter is lined with chairs of leather and metal. The wall and ceiling behind the bar are based on the image of an airplane hangar.

Numerous modern art pieces and abstract paintings have been placed throughout the restaurant. Paintings surrounded by lotus flowers achieve an admirable harmony with the round tables.

A private dining room that seats 18 people can be found in the back of the restaurant. It is well-suited to small parties and radiates a calm luxuriousness. Orient and China House share a kitchen, but Orient features an oriental menu that is a step above that of its downstairs neighbor.

§ ORIENT DATA §

Address: 160 Piccadilly London W1 UK　Phone: 020-74996888

Interior designer: Fusion(Sophie Douglas)

Opening date: March 2000　Seats: 140

Average Price for lunch: 20pounds　Average Price for dinner: 35pounds

1st.	レセプション	Reception
2nd.	エントランス左側にあるギフトショップ	Souvenir shop
3rd.	赤い柱が印象的なダイニング全景	A whole view of the main dining

1st.	重厚なつくりのエントランス	Entrance
2nd.	エントランス右側にあるチャイナバー	Bar

CHINA HOUSE
Chinese restaurant/London

§ CHINA HOUSE DATA §

Address: 160 Piccadilly London W1 UK   Phone: 020-74996996
Interior designer: Fusion(Sophie Douglas)   Opening date: March 2000   Seats: 165
Average Price for lunch: 15pounds   Average Price for dinner: 25pounds

リッツホテルの隣にある、最近まで銀行があったビルが大改装され、2000年の中国の旧正月に中国料理店として営業を開始した。この建物は1920年代に建築家のWilliam Curtis Greenによって自動車のショールームとして設計され、1927年からは銀行となっていたところで、東西のインテリアの融合をコンセプトとしてレストランへの変身が試みられた。

エントランス左側には、オリエンタル情緒あふれるギフトショップがあり、右側はチャイナバー、正面がレストランという配置で、高さ9mのアーチ型天井を支えるように朱色の柱が白と黒の大理石の床の上に取り付けられた。

馬蹄形をした銀行のカウンターはレストランの長イスとなり、わずかに当時の雰囲気を残している。ランチは15ポンド前後で、アフタヌーンティーを楽しむ婦人も多い。ディナーは新しい中国のムードを求める若者に人気がある。ロンドンには2000軒以上もの中国料理店があるといわれるが、このレストランは最もヨーロッパに溶け込んだレストランといえそうである。

China House opened on New Year's Day 2000 on the Chinese lunar calendar in an extensively remodeled former bank next to the hotel The Ritz. Architect William Curtis Green designed this building in the 1920s as an automobile showroom. It was a bank from 1927 until its conversion into China House, the interior design of which fuses East and West.

To the left of the entrance is a gift shop that overflows with the feel of the Orient. To the right of the entrance is a Chinese bar, and the restaurant is straight ahead. A scarlet pillar on the black-and-white marble floor supports the 9-meter, arched ceiling.

In the restaurant, the horseshoe-shaped counter of the bank has been converted into elongated seating, which helps China House maintain a little of its former atmosphere. Lunch costs about £15. A large number of women patronize China House for afternoon tea. At dinner time, the restaurant is popular with young people seeking a new kind of Chinese ambiance.

London is said to be home to more than 2,000 Chinese restaurants, but this may be the one that best blends in with its European surroundings.

客席全景　A whole view of the restaurant

PANAMA
Restaurant/Amsterdam

PANAMAは開発が進むアムステルダム中央駅から東側の地区、イースタン・ドックランドにある。1880年に竣工した総面積1500㎡のパワーステーション（発電施設）を改装しオープンした。アムステルダムで最近特に注目されているスポットで、レセプションを中心にレストラン、カフェ、ライブシアター、バー、ディスコなどがある。

ここで紹介するレストランは240㎡の120席、レセプションからガラススクリーン越しにアプローチされている。夏の間はアウトドア席が格好のリゾート気分を醸し出す。高い天井からは、メタルフレームに裸電球を取り付けたシャンデリアが2つ吊されており、1940年代を彷彿し、ノスタルジーをかき立てる。奥の厨房の上部にあるメザニンはパーティー用のダイニングルームに使用され、新築ビルのレストランでは経験できないノスタルジックな開放感を味わうことができる。

Panama is located in the Eastern Dockland district on the east side of the still-developing Amsterdam central station. The restaurant opened in a 1,500-square-meter remodeled power station building, which was completed in 1880. The building has been the object of a particularly large amount of attention lately in Amsterdam. It is dominated by a reception area, but also features a cafe, a live theater, a bar and a disco.

The restaurant is 240square meters with 120 seats.During the summer, the outdoor seating engenders a resort ambiance.With two metal-framed chandeliers bearing naked light bulbs hanging from the high ceiling, the restaurant resembles an eatery from the 1940s. Above the kitchen, which is located in the back, is a mezzanine used for patio dining rooms, the openness of which gives diners a taste of nostalgia that cannot be found in a restaurant in a new building.

建物全景　Facade　　　メザニンに設置された照明器具　Lighting fixture of the mezzanine

壁際のソファ席　Dining Table　　　ドリンクカウンター　Counter

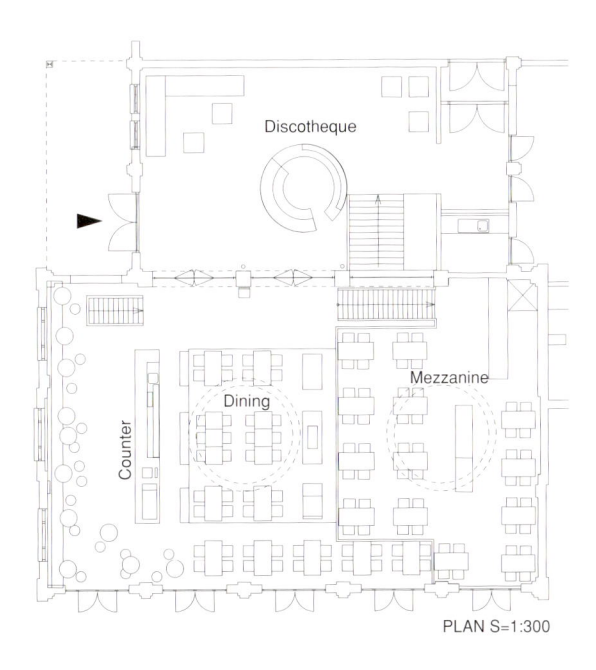

PLAN S=1:300

§ PANAMA DATA §

Address: Oostelijke Handelskade 4 1019 BM Amsterdam Netherlands

Phone: 020-3118680　Interior designer: Bureau Vasd

Opening date: 22th. March 2001　Building Area: 1500m² Restaurant 240m²

Seats: 120　Average Price for lunch: 10euroes　Average Price for dinner: 35euroes

本格的なフランス料理が供されるレストラン　Dining of the restaurant

CLUB GASCON
Restaurant & Pub/London

パブ全景　Pub　　　パブのカウンター　Counter of the pub　　　レストランのカウンター　Counter of the restaurant

パブ最奥のコーナーの客席　Table and chair of the pub

CLUB GASCONは、ロンドンの台所を預かる中央市場に隣接するウエストスミス・フィールドにある。フレンチグルメ愛好者が集うクラブが経営するレストランで、CellarとよばれるパブとClubレストランの2つに分かれている。

Cellarの方は重厚なインテリアで、入り口の右側にはレザーウオールがあり、カウンターにはレザーとメタルのイスが並び、高級なフランスのモダンパブ、80年代のイメージである。他方、Clubレストランは白大理石を使い、本格的なフランス料理を提供、シーフードも好評であるという。バーカウンターの奥にはメタル製のワインセラーがあり、在庫状況の確認や管理を容易にするアイデアが施されている。ロンドン在住のフランス料理通の人たちの人気を得ている。

Club Gascon is located in West Smithfield, which is adjacent to the Central Market that keeps the kitchens of London well-supplied. Managed by a club where devotees of French gourmet food gather, Club Gascon is divided into a pub called Cellar and a restaurant known as Club.

To the right of the entrance to Cellar's dignified interior is a leather wall. Featuring a bar lined with leather-and-metal chairs, it achieves the image of a high-grade French bar of the 1980s. Club is decorated with white marble and serves authentic French food. The seafood is also said to be excellent. A metal wine cellar is found behind the bar counter, and the owners have implemented a number of ideas for easily checking and maintaining its inventory. Club Gascon has found popularity among London's resident French cuisine experts.

§ CLUB GASCON DATA §

Address: 57 West Smithfield London EC1 UK　Phone: 020-77960600
Interior designer: Sophie Douglas
Opening date: Cellar 13th. March 2000　Club 13th. September 1998
Building Area: Cellar 90m^2　Club 120m^2　Seats: Cellar 40　Club 60　Average Price for lunch: Cellar15pounds Club 45pounds
Average Price for dinner: Cellar15pounds Club 45pounds　Business hours: 12:00~22:30

バーカウンターへのアプローチ　Bar counter　　　バンケットルーム　Banquet room

客席。テームズ川の眺望を配慮して通路より一段上がっている　Dining　　　客席とテームズ川　Dining table and Thames River

NEAT
French restaurant/London

オクソタワーに2001年6月1日にオープンした高級フランス料理店NEATは、ミシュラン2スターシェフ、リチャード・ニート氏が経営するレストランである。

店の形はテームズ川に面した横長で、それを生かすべく窓は開放的なつくりになっている。ブラッスリー100席、バンケットルーム20席、レストラン120席が配置されている。ブラッスリーはラベンダー色のソファ席で、背後にはブロンズ色の壁があり、プロバンス風の色彩をイメージしている。レストラン席にはわずかであるが床に段差を設け、テームズ川の眺望を考慮した設計となっている。

客席は余裕があり快適で、その豪華さは他のレストランとは比較できない感じである。ブラッスリーのランチセットは29ポンド、レストランでのディナーは49ポンドと、かなり高価である。

Michelin two-star chef Richard Neat manages the upscale French restaurant Neat, which opened in Oxo Tower on June 1, 2001.

The oblong restaurant faces the Thames River and incorporates expansive windows to take advantage of this fact. Neat is made up of a 100-seat brasserie, a 20-seat banquet room and a 120-seat main restaurant. The brasserie features lavender sofas backed by bronze-colored walls, creating a Provençal color scheme. The main restaurant's seating area was designed with slight differences in floor level in consideration of the view of the Thames.

Each seat is given a comfortable amount of extra space, creating a luxuriousness that seems incomparable to any other restaurant. Neat is fairly expensive, as demonstrated by the price of the lunch set: £29 in the brasserie and £49 in the main restaurant.

§ NEAT DATA §
Address: OXO Tower Wharf. Bargehouse Street London SE1 UK　Phone: 020-79285533
Interior designer: Sophie Neat　Kieran Curtis　Opening date: 1st. June 2001
Building Area: 900m²　Seats: 250
Average Price for lunch: 29pounds　Average Price for dinner: 49pounds

バーカウンター　Bar counter

FOCUS

コンクリート（CONCRETE ARCHITECTURAL ASSOCIATES）は、デザイナーGilian Schrofer、インテリア・アーキテクトEric von Dillen、それにアーキテクトRob Wegemansによって1997年に設立されたデザインスタジオで、ヘッドオフィスをアムステルダムに置き、現在スタッフを含めて総勢12人からなるクリエーター集団である。

結成後わずか4年という短い期間ではあるが、後のページで紹介するSUPPER CLUB（80ページ）やCOFFEE COMPANY（86ページ）など、飲食空間をメーンに年間40～50件のプロジェクトをこなし、その活躍ぶりには"勢い"が感じられる。リーダーの一人であるGilian Schroferは、コンクリートの特筆すべきコンセプトとして「われわれのプロジェクトに対して、魅力的か否かという議論をよく耳にするが、それはあくまでも個人的な見解やセンスの問題であって、最終的には商業的な成功を収めなければ意味がない」と強調し、その徹底ぶりは各プロジェクトの中に浸透している。また、Rob Wegemansは「われわれの各プロジェクトのクリエーションの深さを見てほしい」と語る。

成功への取っ掛かりとなったSUPPER CLUBを見てみると、吹き抜けの空間に入ったとたん、まずはその空間構成の大胆さに驚かされる。ここでは一日に起こったこと、世俗のことをしばし忘れてしまうような雰囲気が十分にある。オランダにはクツを脱ぎマットレスに座って飲食する習慣が過去にあったのだろうか。これは完全にアジア、東洋のスタイルを演出したキッチュに違いないが、そこには大胆さといやしさを求めて、連日多くの人が集い、予約が取れないほどの繁盛ぶりである。

店内には、両サイドにバルコニーが広い空間を包み込むかのように設置さ

Concrete Architectural Associates is a design studio founded by designer Gilian Schrofer, interior architect Eric von Dillen and architect Rob Wegemans in 1997. Its head office is in Amsterdam and its staff consists of 12 creative individuals.

Only four years have passed since Concrete's formation, but the studio has completed between 40 and 50 projects a year, the bulk of which have been eating and drinking establishments such as Supper Club (Page 80) and Coffee Company (Page 86). It is quite an impressive pace.

An idea put forward by Schrofer deserves special mention: "We often hear people discussing whether our projects are appealing, but that is a matter of individual viewpoint and sensibility. Unless a project is commercially successful, such questions are ultimately meaningless." This attitude of thoroughness permeates every project. Wegemans adds, "I want people to look at the depth of our projects."

At Supper Club, which set Concrete on the path to success, from the moment one enters the well, he is struck by the boldness of the spatial composition. The atmosphere allows one to easily forget for a moment the day's events and the outside world. Do you suppose there was once a Dutch custom of removing one's shoes and eating and drinking while sitting on a mattress? Supper Club is just a kitschy reproduction of Asian custom. But every day the boldness and sheer crassness of the concept attracts so many customers it is impossible to get a reservation.

Inside, the balcony seems to envelop the large space from each side.

CONCRETE

れている。ここへ一人で来ようが、何人で来ようが、また、知人はもちろんのこと見知らぬ他人であっても皆一緒であるというフレンドシップの発想が潜んでいる。

キッチンからダイニングスペースへは、とくにウエーター用の通路は設けられておらず、バルコニーへの専用階段もない。レジカウンターのところにはバルコニーから手が届く位置にテーブルを設け、ウエーターが背伸びをして料理や飲み物を手渡しているシーンを目にするとき、そこには忘れがたい、プリミティブなユーモアを発見することができる。

彼らのデザインの特長として、SUPPER CLUBやCOFFEE COMPANYに見られる、光の変化による効果も見逃せない。光に映像や音楽をミックスした空間づくりは感動を与えると同時に、トレンドを先取りするかのような重要な構成要因といえる。

*

これまでリーダーたちのコンビネーションがうまく絡み合い、高い評価を得て成功を収めてきているが、彼らはこの状態が永遠に続くとは思っていないようだ。皆それぞれに将来はアーティストとして独立を夢見ており、コンテンポラリーなパートナーとしての現実を自覚しているという。「コンクリートでの実績は、ポートフォリオとなることは間違いない」とGilian Schroferは語る。

SUPPER CLUBはアムステルダム、ロンドン、ローマに出店されているが、第4号店の候補地として日本をターゲットにしているという。日本に出店した場合、果たしてどういうリアクションが期待できるのであろうか。彼らの今後の活動に注目したい。

Whether one comes alone or in a group, the idea of camaraderie with other patrons, be they acquaintances or strangers, partly explains Supper Club's success.

No corridor leads from the kitchen to the dining space, and no staircase leads to the balconies. In the cash register counter area, a table has been placed in a spot within reach of the balcony. The sight of the wait staff standing on tiptoe to pass dishes and drinks back and forth provides a primitive humor not easily forgotten.

In searching for the strengths in Concrete's designs, one cannot overlook the changing light effects of Supper Club and Coffee Company. These effects not only carry the impact of mixing light, video and music, but also seem to preview trends.

*

Based on the reception they've received, Concrete's combination of leaders has so far been a success. They, however, seem to think the current situation will not last. Each of them dreams of becoming an independent artist, and they say they are self-conscious about their current status as partners. "There is no doubt that my accomplishments at Concrete contribute to my portfolio," says Schrofer.

Supper Club has outlets in Amsterdam, London and Rome, and Concrete has its sights set on Japan for a fourth location. If they did create a Japan restaurant, what kind of reception do you suppose it would receive? It will be interesting to watch what Concrete does in the future.

両サイドがバルコニーとなった1階客席全景　Dining of the first floor

SUPPER CLUB

地下1階ラウンジのソファ席の色の変化の様子
A change of the light of the lounge on basement

Nightclub/Amsterdam

ディシャップカウンター兼用の1階バーカウンター　Bar counter

地下1階ラウンジ　Lounge of the basement

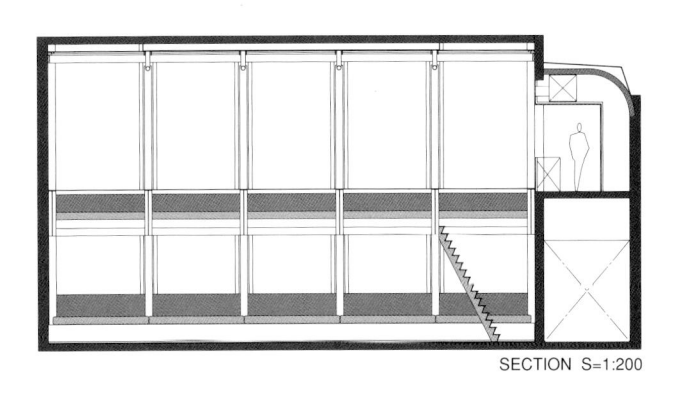

SECTION S=1:200

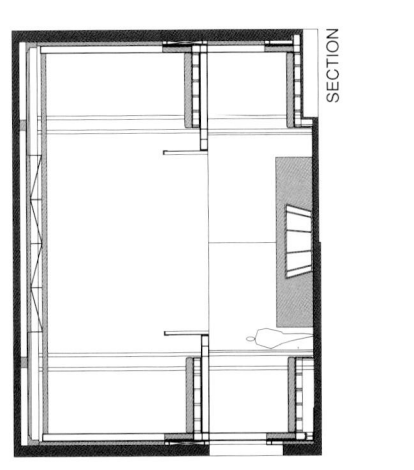

SECTION

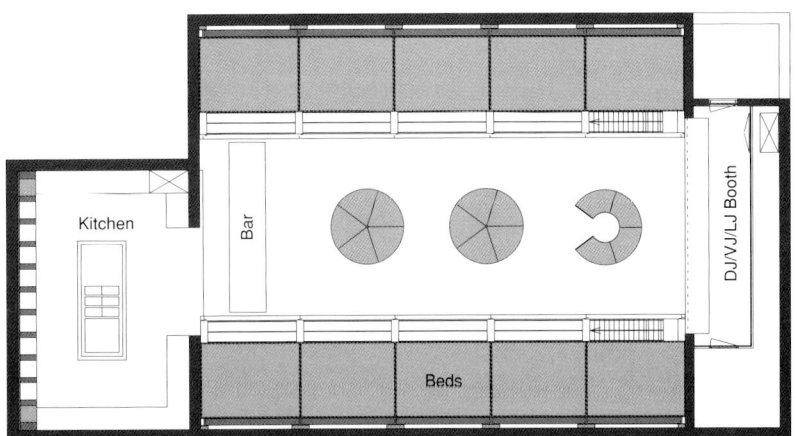

Kitchen | Bar | DJ/VJ/LJ Booth

Beds

1F PLAN S=1:200

SECTION S=1:200

SECTION

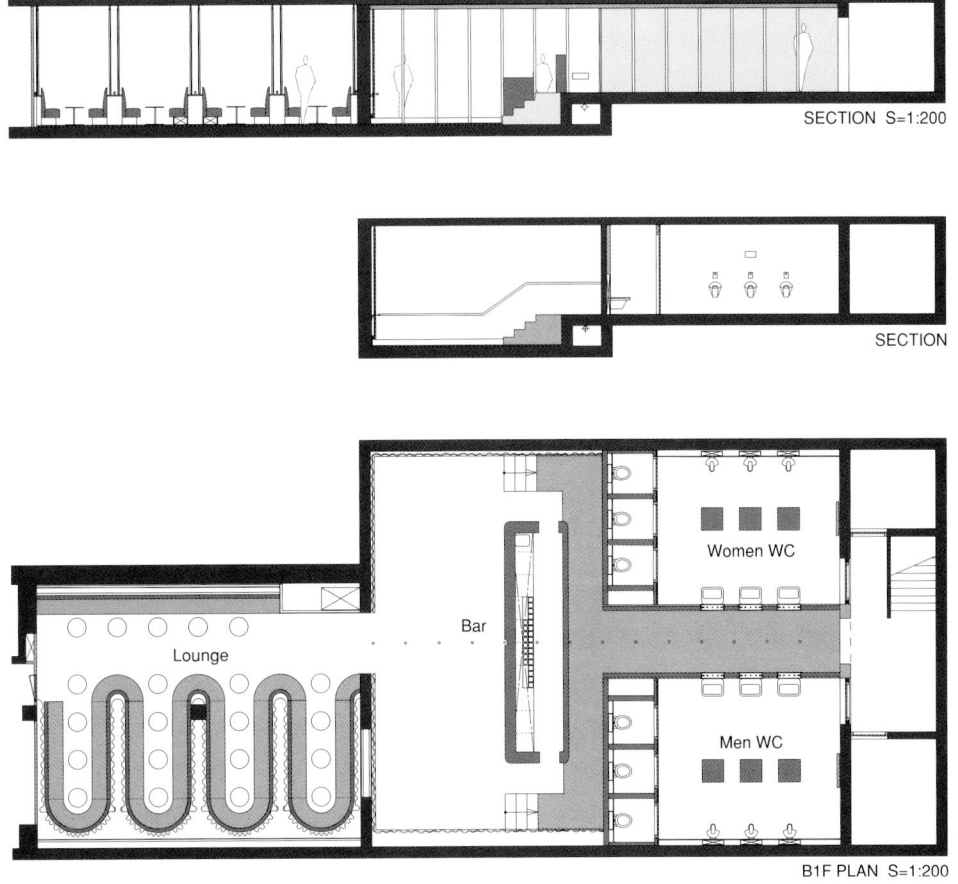

Lounge | Bar | Women WC | Men WC

B1F PLAN S=1:200

83

1999年10月にオープンしたSUPPER CLUBは、コンクリートの出世作の一つで、話題を振りまいたアーティスティックなレストランである。週末、平日にかかわらず、開店の8時を過ぎると客が続々と詰めかけ、マットレスにクッションが置いてある座席に、クツを脱いで案内される。ヨーロッパでは見かけない風景である。ダンスフロアともなる中央の吹き抜け空間の両サイドがバルコニーで、厨房は奥にある。スクリーンには興味を引かれるようなイメージやカラー映像が映し出される。映像は日替わりである。白いマットレスに座って飲んで食べて、ここではマッサージもリクエストできるので、心身ともにリラックスできる。

地下にはラウンジがあり、空間のカラーが照明によって6通りに自動的に変化しムードを高める。トイレにもユーモアがあり、ヘテロ、ホモ用に分かれて設置されている。さらに洗面器の前のミラーはツーウエイ方式で、通路を通る人は内側で化粧をする女性の様子を観察できる。このSUPPER CLUBはロンドン、ローマでも同じコンセプトで建設中である。

Supper Club, which opened in October 1999, is one of the famous creations of Concrete Architectural Associates. The reputation of this artistic restaurant has spread far and wide.

On both weekends and weekdays, from its 8 p.m. opening, the restaurant is constantly packed with customers, who are asked to remove their shoes and then led to seats consisting of cushions on mattresses. It is a scene seldom seen in Europe. There is a balcony on either side of the central well, which also serves as a dance floor. The kitchen is in the back. Interesting images and colorful figures are projected on a screen. These images change every day. While sitting on a white mattress eating and drinking, customers can also request a massage, allowing them to relax both their bodies and minds.

In the basement salon, lights cast a succession of six different colors of light, elevating the mood. For a humorous touch, the restrooms are labeled "heterosexual" and "homosexual." The mirrors in the restrooms are two-way, permitting people passing by in the corridor to see women inside doing their makeup.

Supper Clubs are also under construction in London and Rome.

1st.	1階ホール中央のテーブル席	Dining table
2nd.	バーカウンター	Bar counter
3rd.	クツを脱いで上がる座席	Sit-down floor
4th.	地下1階トイレの洗面所	Restroom of the basement

§ SUPPER CLUB DATA §

Address: Jonge Roelensteeg 21 1012 PL Amsterdam Netherlands

Phone: 020-3446404

Architect+Design: Concrete Architectural Associates

Opening date: October 1999

Building Area: 150m²   Seats: 160

Average Price for dinner: 175guilders

地下1階男性・女性トイレに挟まれた通路。壁の窓からは洗面所のミラーを通して内部の様子が見える。洗面所側からは通路側が見えない。Passage of the basement

COFFEE COMPANY

店内全景。木製のロングテーブルと色分けされたサンプルケースが空間のポイント　A whole view of the shop

コーヒー豆のサンプルのディスプレイ　Display of the sample

多くの色を使いながらモノトーンの空間と不思議にマッチしているサンプルケース
Display of the sample

カウンター背後のメニューボード。ドリンク類の詳細な説明もある　Menu board

アムステルダム市内で現在8店舗を展開しているCOFFEE COMPANYは「コーヒーと香りと色」を基本コンセプトに、コンクリートがデザイン・開発しているフランチャイズ店である。店の規模は小さいが、色分けしたコーヒーショーケースを設置し、通行客が通りからアイキャッチできるような強力なカラーによるインパクトの強さを売り物にしている。

この店は最新のもので、市の中心から西側に延びる商店街・ハーレマーディークにある。店内には木製のロングテーブルが置いてあり、勝手に座り会話を交わし、庶民的な気楽さを求められているような自由な雰囲気が漂う。注文カウンターでは、価格やメニューを分かりやすくイラスト付きで表示しているのも親しみを感じさせる。

Coffee Company is a franchise chain with eight outlets in Amsterdam that was designed and developed by Concrete Architectural Associates based on the concept of "coffee, its aroma and its color." The shops have limited space, but they make effect use of it by putting color-coded coffee showcases inside. Their high-impact colors effectively catch the eyes of passers-by.

This shop is the newest, and it is located in the Haarlemmerdijk commercial district that stretches westward from the city center. A long, wooden table inside the shop helps create a free, informal and plebeian atmosphere that invites customers to sit and chat. The illustrated, easy-to-understand price display by the order counter adds to the friendliness of this Coffee Company location.

§ COFFEE COMPANY DATA §

Address: Haarlemmerdijk 62 1013 JE Amsterdam Netherlands
Phone: 020-6263776
Architect+Design: Concrete Architectural Associates
Opening date: May 2000　Building Area: 70m²　Seats: 25

最奥のクラブからレストラン客席を見る　Dining of the restaurant

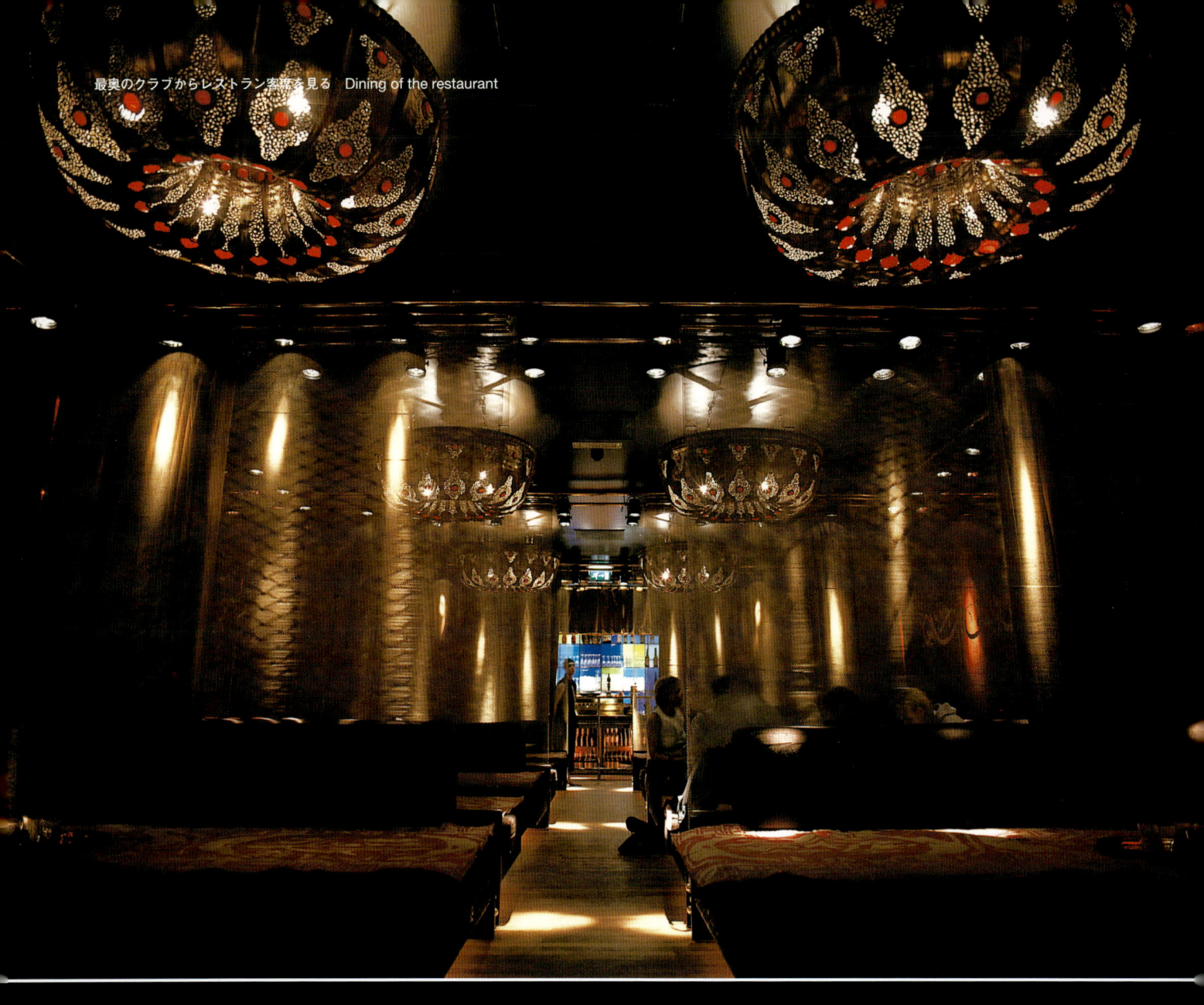

NORMADS

コンクリートのオフィスが入っているビルの1階にオープンした、アラブ風レストラン+ナイトクラブである。「東西の出会い」をコンセプトにしたNORMADSは、オランダ人がクリエートするアラブ風のメッカにふさわしい雰囲気に満ちている。

入り口近くの窓際には、ブルーを基調にしたカラーガラスで演出されたバーがあり、中央はレストランになっている。通路に沿って左右に真鍮のテーブルをコの字形に囲んだ座席がある。Kelimと呼ばれるミニカーペットを敷き、背もたれにクッションを置き、半透明のスクリーンを吊し隣との間仕切りとしている。天井からはデザイナー自らモロッコに出向き指示して作ったという、メタリックのアラビアンランプが妖しい光を放つ。アラブ通のためのクイジーヌを目指すシェフ、Quadeer Rehmani氏の本格的な料理はオープン早々話題となり、ファッションデザイナーAzizによるユニフォームを身に付けたウエーターが店内の雰囲気を大いに盛り上げている。

バーカウンターから見るレストラン。アラブ風のしつらえ　Dining of the restaurant

Arabian restaurant&Nightclub/Amsterdam

This Arabian restaurant and nightclub is located on the first floor of the building that houses Concrete Architectural Associates. Normads, with its "East meets West" concept, is full of atmosphere befitting an Arabian Mecca created by the Dutch.

By the window near the entrance is a bar featuring blue-based colored glass, and in the center of Normads is the restaurant. Seats surrounded by brass tables in the shape of an angular letter c have been placed to the left and right along a passageway. The ground is covered with miniature carpets called "kelim," and cushions are used as backrests; semitransparent screens are hung as partitions. Metallic Arabian lamps, the making of which the designer personally oversaw in Morocco, hang from the ceiling, casting a peculiar light.

The authentic cooking of chef Quadeer Rehmani, who aims for a cuisine to please people well versed in Arab culture, was much talked about from the minute Normads opened. Waiters wearing uniforms designed by fashion designer Aziz contribute much to the restaurant's ambiance.

バーカウンター　Bar counter

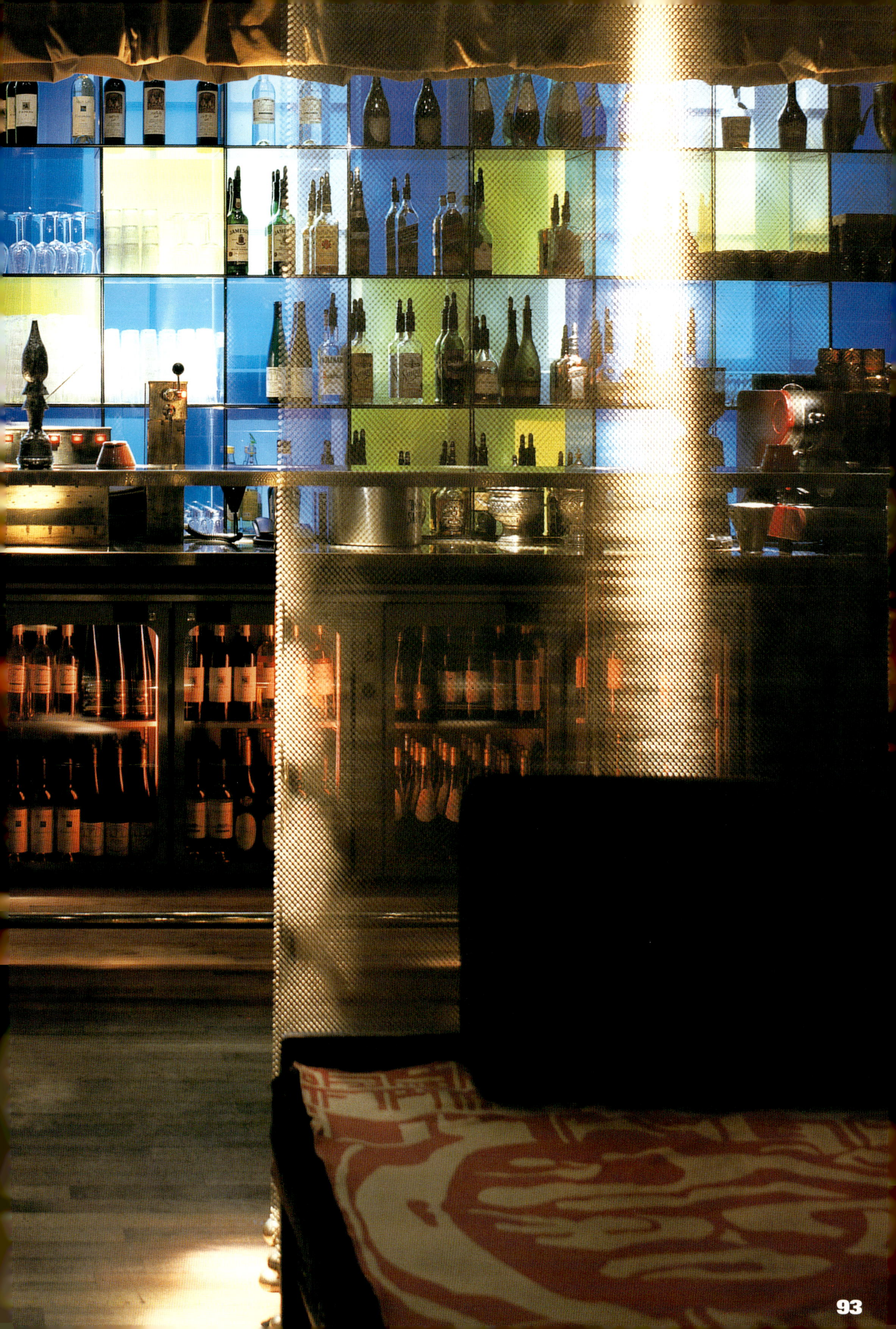

ファサード　Facade　　　　　　　　　最奥のクラブのダンスフロア　Club

レストラン客席　Dining of the restaurant

クラブへの通路の壁面の照明　Lighting fixture of the passage

客席を緩やかに仕切る半透明のスクリーン　Screen

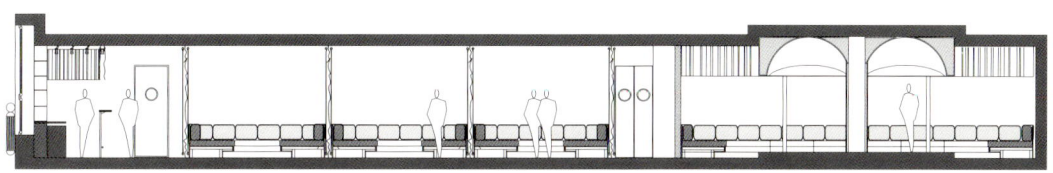

SECTION S=1:200

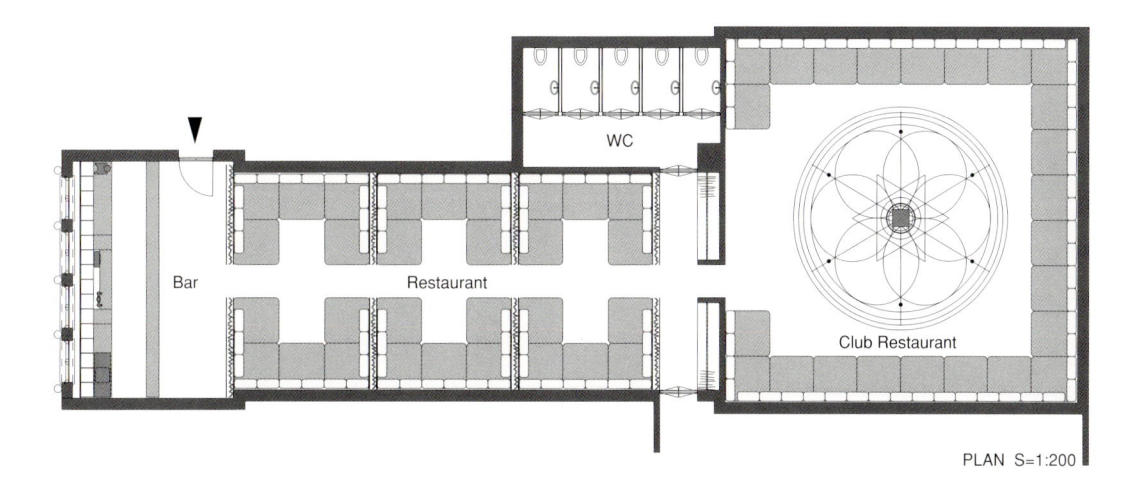

PLAN S=1:200

§ NORMADS DATA §

Address: Rozengracht 133 1016 LV Amsterdam Netherlands

Phone: 020-3446401

Architect+Design: Concrete Architectural Associates

Opening date: May 2001　Building Area: 200m²　Seats: 140

Average Price for dinner: 99guilders

ファサード　Facade

LAUNDRY INDUSTRY

LAUNDRY INDUSTRY

入り口まわり。店内奥に向かって傾斜させている様子が分かる　Entrance

天井の照明の色はプログラミングされており、6つの色に変化　Facade

LAUNDRY INDUSTRYは10年前にアムステルダムで創設されたファッションブランドで、このノッティンヒル店はロンドン進出の2番めの店で、このほかにベルリンにも専門ショップを持つ。ターゲットとしては25歳から30歳くらいのカジュアルラインである。

ストレートな店内は、外からでは分からない程度に道路側から4度の傾斜が付けられており、中央には段差を設け、両サイドはスロープという設計となっている。気分的に平衡感覚に疑いを持つ程度の不安定さは感じる。天井からの光はコンピューター制御で6色に変化し、ミュージックと光による感動的なインテリアを演出する。黒く覆った天井のラインは売り場と強力なコントラストをなす。エントランス左側はハンガーシステムが奥まで続き、右側はコンクリート打ち放しの3枚のディスプレイボードを配し、同素材でレジカウンターを設置し、木目を生かして素材感を強調している。

Laundry Industry is a fashion brand established in Amsterdam 10 years ago. This Notting Hill shop is the brand's second specialty store and first in London; there is another in Berlin. The casual clothing line is aimed at people around the 25-to-30 age range.

Though you can't tell by looking from outside, the interior inclines downward about four degrees from the street. A step has been created in the center, with a slope on each side. The design creates a feeling of instability.

The computer-controlled lights on the ceiling rotate among six different colors. Together with the music, they create an exciting interior. The all-black ceiling and sales floor combine to create a powerful design concept. A hanger system stretches from the left of the entrance to the back of the shop. To the right are three concrete-finish display boards. With the cash register counter made of the same material, the design emphasizes the texture of the material.

レジカウンター　Cashier

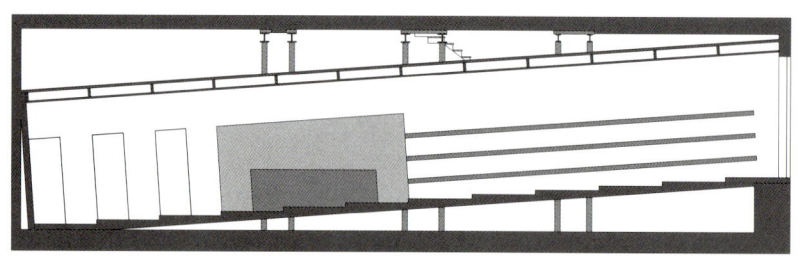

SECTION S=1:200

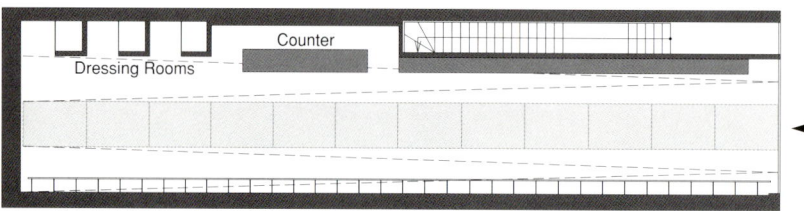

Dressing Rooms　Counter

PLAN S=1:200

店内奥より入り口方向を見る　A whole view of the shop

§ LAUNDRY INDUSTRY DATA §

Address: 186 Westbourne Grove W11 London UK　Phone: 020-77927967

Architect+Design: Concrete Architectural Associates

Opening date: April 2000　Building Area: 80m²

Business hours: 12:00~18:00 (Mon.)　10:00~19:00 (Tue.~Sat.)　11:00~20:00 (Thu.)

RITUALS

アクリル板にネオンを内蔵したディスプレイ棚　Display shelf

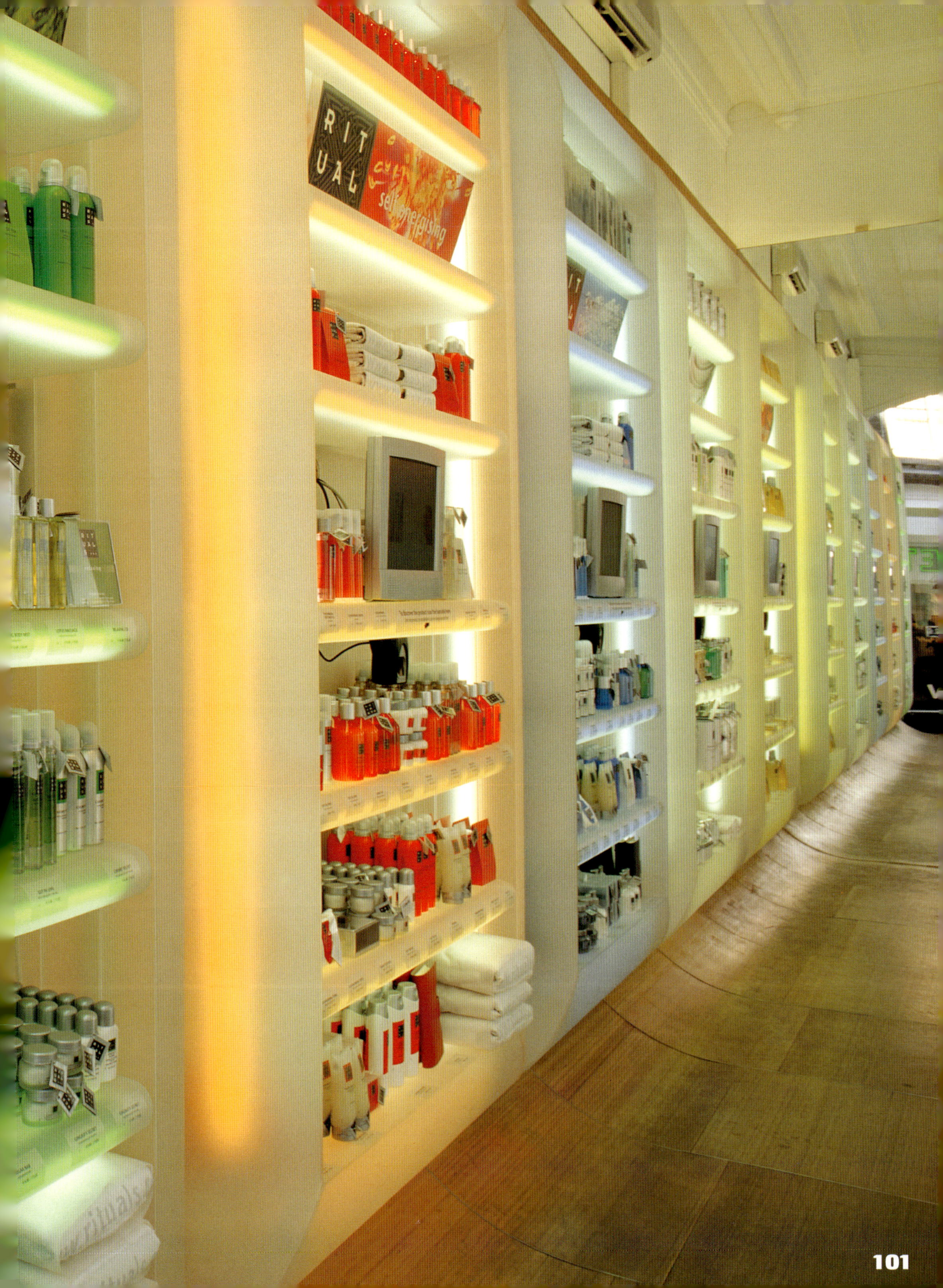
RIT
UAL

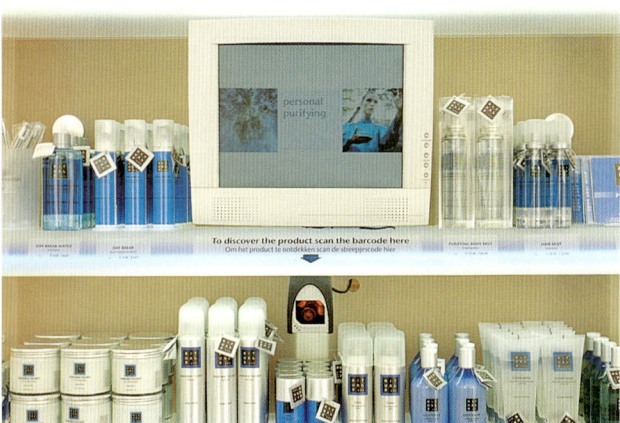

RITUALSはオランダのナチュラルコスメティックの最新ブランドで、この店は第1号店となる。2000年11月、アムステルダムで最もにぎわいを見せるショッピング街・カルフアー通りに開店した。

「ボディとホーム（家庭）に清潔なプロダクトを販売するスペース」をコンセプトに、コンクリートが手掛けたものである。店内に入ると正面には色ごとに商品が分類され、それらがネオンを内蔵した棚に整然と納められている。棚の中央にはモニターがあり、商品のバーコードをセンサーに近づけると、その商品の詳細なインフォメーションがモニター上に現れる。バンブー（竹）製の合板で一体化された壁は、カーブを描いてフロアに連なっており、清涼感がある。バンブーを使った床もたいへん珍しい。店内奥にはボディケアを実演するアクアバッグも置かれている。

今後、フル回転して全国に販売網を築いていくということである。日曜日も営業し、定休日はなしである。

Rituals is Holland's newest brand of natural cosmetics, and this is its first store. It opened on Kalver Street, the most bustling shopping street in Amsterdam, in November 2000.

Rituals was built by Concrete Architectural Associates based on the concept of a space for selling products that bring cleanliness to both the body and the home. The products inside the shop are well organized and categorized by color on shelves that have built-in neon lights. In the center of each shelf is a monitor. Bringing the bar code on a product near the monitor causes detailed information about the product to be displayed.

The curved, bamboo-veneer-board-covered walls have a refreshing quality, and the bamboo floor is also a rarity. Water resistant bags for body care are found in the back.

Rituals plans to build a nationwide sales network. The store is open every day of the week.

1st.　店内中央から奥を見る　A back room of the shop
2nd.　ディスプレイ棚に設置されたモニター　Monitor
3rd.　商品のバーコードをセンサーに近づけると、その商品の詳細なインフォメーションがモニター上に現れる
　　　Monitor shows the information of the commodity
4th.　アクアケア用品のディスプレイ　Aquacare corner

入り口　Entrance

入り口から店内を見る　A whole view of the shop

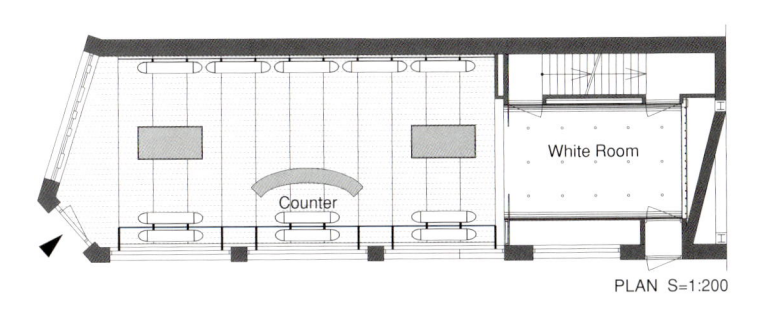

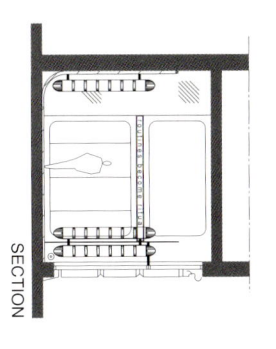

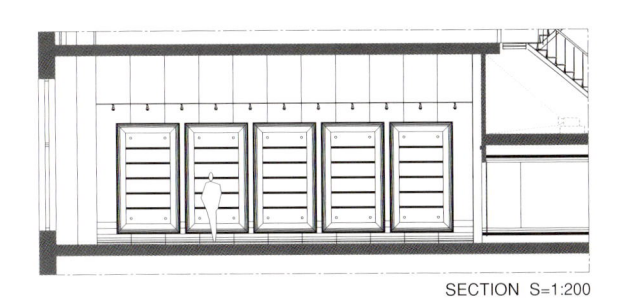

PLAN　S=1:200

SECTION

SECTION　S=1:200

§ RITUALS DATA §

Address: Kalverstraat 73 1012 NZ Amsterdam Netherlands　Phone: 020-3449221

Architect+Design: Concrete Architectural Associates

Opening date: November 2000　Building Area: 75m²　Seats: 140

Business hours: 10:00~18:00 (Mon.)　9:00~18:00 (Tue.~Sat.)　12:00~18:00 (Sun.)

BLENDER

入り口から見た中央のカウンターと客席　A view of the dining from the entrance

バーカウンター　Bar counter

Restaurant/Amsterdam

スタルクのイスが並べられたテラス席　Outdoor section

運河に面した建物外観　Facade

レストランのカウンターに置かれた卵形のランプ　Lamp

市の中心から西へ2キロほどの、カッテンスロート運河沿いに新しく開発された高級住宅街の一角に2000年12月にオープンしたレストランである。建物の形状が扇形のため、インテリアはユニークな空間構成が試みられた。

バーコーナーの背後にレストランとカウンターがある設計で、シェフはバー内で料理をするという珍しいオープン形式のレストランとなっている。その意味で、レストランはバーの一部となっている。レストランのカウンターには卵形のランプが置いてあり、雰囲気を和らげ、落ち着きのあるコーナーを演出する光の間仕切り的存在である。

住宅地にあるため、ランチ時よりも夕方に客は集まる。バーの外にはスタルクのオレンジ色のイスが並び、夏期は住民たちの憩いとコミュニケーションの場として家庭的雰囲気に包まれる。デザイン的には1970年代への回帰といえる。

Blender is a restaurant in a corner of a newly developed, high-grade residential area along the Kattensloot canal about two kilometers west of the city center. Because its building is fan-shaped, the interior has an unusual spatial configuration.

Blender has a rare, open structure in which the restaurant and a counter are behind the bar section, and the chef cooks in the bar. The restaurant can be said to be part of the bar. On the restaurant counter is an egg-shaped lamp, which softens the ambiance and serves as a kind of divider of light to produce a relaxed area.

Because Blender is located in a residential district, it gets more customers at night than during the lunch hour. Starck, orange-colored chairs are lined up outside the bar. Enveloped in a gardenlike ambiance, the spot serves locals as a place for relaxation and communication during the summer. Blender could be called a return to the design of the 1970s.

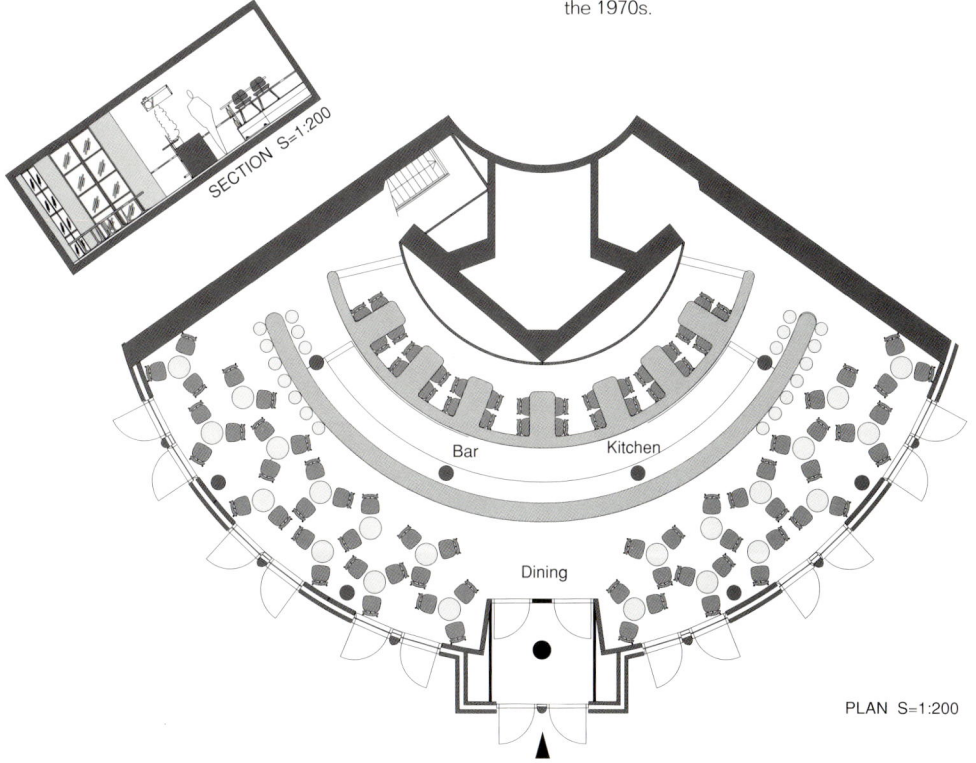

SECTION S=1:200

Bar　Kitchen

Dining

PLAN S=1:200

§ BLENDER DATA §

Address: Van der Paimkade 16 1051 RE Amsterdam Netherlands　Phone: 020-4869860
Architect+Design: Concrete Architectural Associates　Opening date: December 2000
Building Area: 100m^2　Seats: 80　Average Price for dinner: 80guilders

SPRING

オープンキッチン。カウンターの上部にはアルコール、スピリット類のボトルを、下部には自社オリジナルのビン入りのミネラルウオーターを並べている　Kitchen

Restaurant/Amsterdam

キッチン側から見た客席全景　A whole view of the dining

背もたれで二分されている客席　Dining table

フォンデル公園の南側、バスとトラムの停留所のある角地にあるレストランである。外から見ると、フルサイズの窓ガラスを通してレストラン内部がすっぽり一枚の絵のように望める、全44席のワンルームレストランである。

客席は窓辺の中心に花を飾り、その背後からセンターラインとなるハイバックのロングチェアで空間を二分し、両サイドにテーブルを置いた左右対称のダイニングスペースとなっている。厨房も同様に、一枚の絵のように枠組みされた中に納まっている。カウンターの上部にはアルコール、スピリット類のボトルを置き、下部にはオリジナルのビン入りのミネラルウォーターを並べ、調理カウンターを客席から望めるオープン形式になっている。

商店と住宅が渾然一体となった地区にあり、メニューはインターナショナルで、付近の住民を固定客としている。各テーブルにはナプキン、スパイス等を入れる木の箱が置いてある。

The restaurant Spring stands in a corner lot to the south of Vondel Park that also contains a bus and tram stop. All forty four seats in this one-room restaurant can be seen clearly, like a painting, from outside, through the full-size glass window.

Flowers decorate the center of the area near the windows in the seating section. A high-back bench behind them divides the space in two. Tables are placed symmetrically on each side to create a dining area. A wooden box containing napkins, spices and other items has been placed on each table.

The kitchen is also in an area framed like a painting. Bottles of liquor are found above the counter, and original bottled mineral waters are lined up beneath it. The kitchen's open design permits customers to see the cooking counter from their seats.

Spring is in a neighborhood where commercial establishments and residences coexist in complete harmony, and locals are among the regular customers who come to enjoy Spring's international menu.

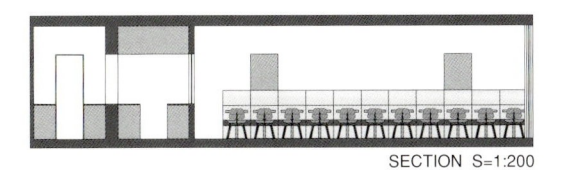

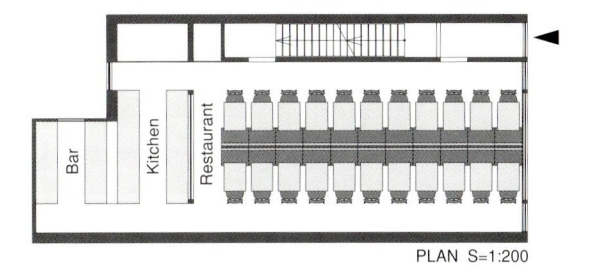

SECTION S=1:200

PLAN S=1:200

§ SPRING DATA §

Address: Willemsparkweg 177 1071 GZ Amsterdam Netherlands　Phone: 020-6754421

Architect+Design: Concrete Architectural Associates

Opening date: May 2000　Building Area: 70m²　Seats: 44

Average Price for lunch: 75guilders　Average Price for dinner: 225guilders

AUSTRALIAN
Ice cream shop/Amsterdam

入り口から見た店内全景　A whole view of the shop

ファサード　Facade

今、オランダの主要都市で人気を博しているのがAUSTRALIANのブランドショップで、アイスクリームとチョコレートの専門店である。その秘訣は純粋な原料を使用していることにある。アイスクリーム職人は朝早くから出勤し、仕込みを入念に行う。

この店舗はシンゲル運河に面し、鋭角の角地に建った細長いビルの1階にある。店内にはアイスクリームとチョコレートを納めたショーケースがあり、床はオーストラリアのイメージでグレーの模様が描かれ、下からオレンジ色の光が当てられ清潔感が漂う。

アイスクリームのコーナーは、ステンレス製の円形の取っ手がついた蓋でグラフィカルにまとめられている。チョコレートは先住民族アボリジニの描く自然と動物をイメージしているようで人気があり、贈答用として受けている。現在アムステルダムに4店、オランダでは30店ほど展開している。

The brand shop Australian, which specializes in ice cream and chocolate, is earning popularity in the Netherlands' main city. Its secret is pure raw materials. The shop's ice cream makers arrive at work early in the morning and begin their careful preparations.

This shop faces the Singel canal from a long, narrow building in an acute-angled corner lot. Inside is a showcase full of ice cream and chocolate. The floor is decorated with a gray pattern that brings to mind Australia, and orange light is shone down on it from above, creating a feeling of cleanliness.

In the ice cream section, varieties are organized in stainless-steel containers with round, handled lids. Australian's popular chocolates are based on Aboriginal drawings of nature and animals, and they are frequently given as gifts.

There are four Australian locations in Amsterdam and 30 in the Netherlands.

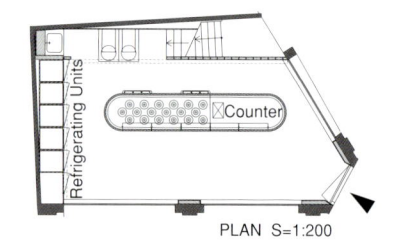

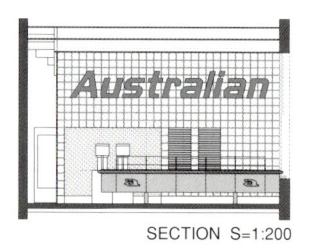

PLAN S=1:200

SECTION S=1:200

§ AUSTRALIAN DATA §

Address: Singel 437 1012 WP Amsterdam Netherlands　Phone: 020-4287533
Architect+Design: Concrete Architectural Associates　Opening date: March 1999　Building Area: 50m²

SPECIALITY STORE & SHOP

強い太陽光を遮るというサングラスのイメージがしつらえられた両サイドの壁　Direction of the wall

ファサード　Facade

B 54 SUN
Sunglasses shop/Berlin

この店はハッケシャー・マルクトに面し、オラニンバーガー通り1番にあるサングラス専門店である。80年代のニューヨークのディスコとして、今や伝説的存在となっている「STUDIO54」をコンセプトに設計されたという。同店はフリードリッヒ通りにもあり、これが2店めになる。

40㎡と店自体は小ぶりであるが、いわゆるデザイナーブランドのメガネをコレクションしており、数も限定されているため、空間には余裕すら感じさせる。店内の照度は高く、カウンターの背後にはバック照明を当て、各ブランドごとにサングラスをガラスプレートに置き浮き立たせている。また、両サイドの壁には市販の円形照明器具を取り付け、透明のレースをドレープ状に吊り下げ、強い太陽光を遮るというサングラスのイメージを作り出している。

ガラスのショーウインドーは設置していないが、道路に面したガラスの内側にガラスプレートを接着しサングラスを置いているところは、ディスプレイ手法として斬新である。

B 54 SUN is a sunglasses shop that faces Hackescher Markt at Oranienburger Str. 1. The shop was designed based on the legendary 1980s New York disco Studio 54. A second B 54 SUN outlet is located on Friedrich Str.

With 40 square meters of floor space, the shop is on the small side, but because it carries only designer-brand sunglasses in limited numbers, the space actually seems more than ample. The interior is well-lighted. The area behind the counter is backlighted, and the sunglasses are arranged on glass plates by brand.

Round lighting equipment designed for marketting sunglasses is attached to the wall on each side and transparent lace has been hung like drapes. These two design elements create an image reminiscent of sunglasses blocking bright sunlight.

The shop has no glass display window, but the owners have overcome this limitation by placing sunglasses on a glass plate attached to the inside of the window facing the road.

Christian Dior

CHANEL

EMPORIO ARMANI

メジャーブランドのサングラスが飾られているディスプレイ棚　Detail of the display shelf

ガラスプレートをファサードのガラス面に接着したディスプレイ台
Display shelf

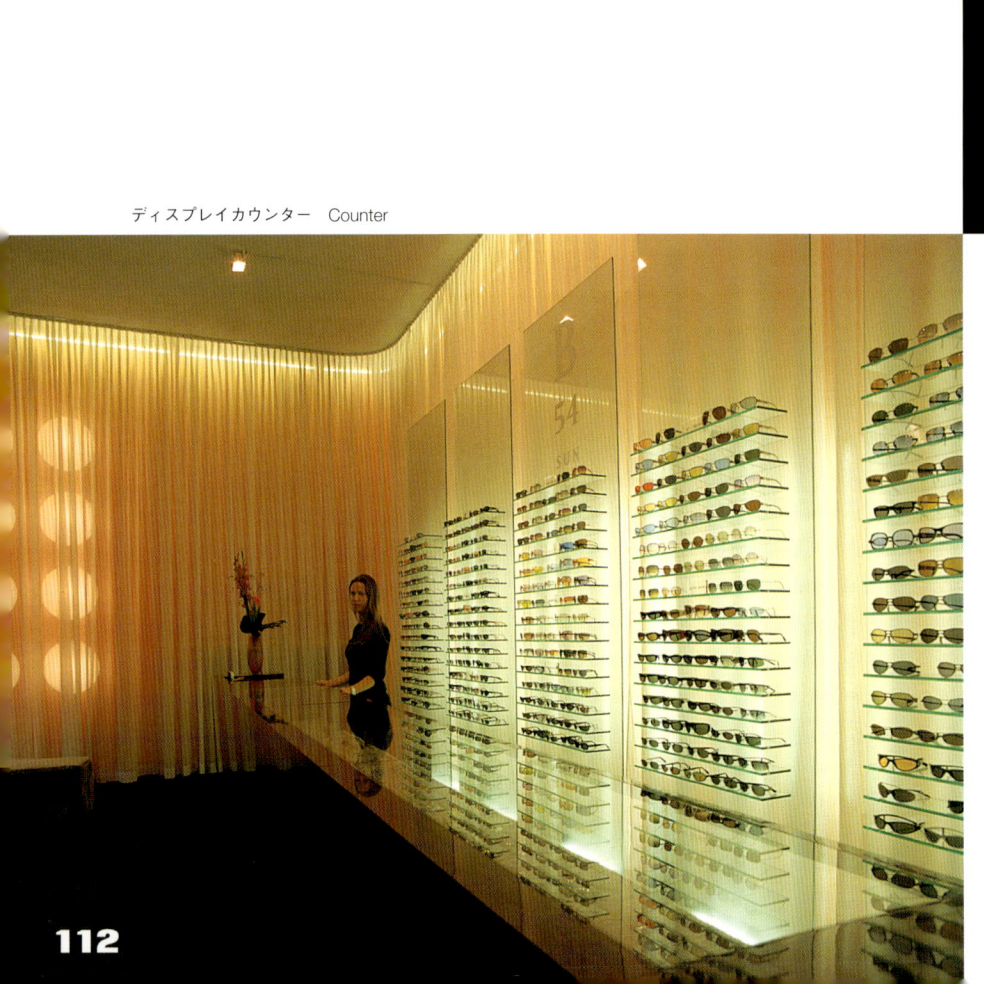

ディスプレイカウンター　Counter

ディスプレイ棚全景　A whole view of the display shelf

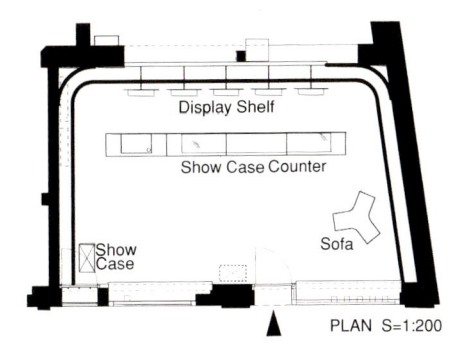

§ B 54 SUN DATA §

Address: Oranienburger Str. 1 10707 Berlin Germany　Phone: 030-28040818

Architect+Design: Player&Franz Studio　Building Area: 40m²

Business hours: 11:00~20:00 (Mon.~Fri.)　11:00~16:00 (Sat.)

シルバー1色で構成されたフィッティングルーム　Dressing room

MOUDJAHIDIN
Boutique/Paris

1st.　エントランスのサイン　Sign
2nd.　最奥のレディスのコーナー。フィッティングルームとそのデザインに対応した天井のデザイン
　　　Back room

レジ前から店内奥を見る　A view of the shop from the cashier

観光客や買い物客で常ににぎわいを見せるレ・アールに開店したこのMOUDJAHIDINは、アラブ風インテリアのヒップ・ホップ・ファッションのブティックである。エントランスにはレジと男性の売り場があり、中央にミニサロンとシューズ売り場、フィッティングルーム、奥はレディスという構成で、ミュージックに乗って踊るスペースも十分にあり、ミラーを多く配置するとともに、モスクに象徴されるようなデコレーションが店内のムードを高めている。

シューズのディスプレイは水道管とアルミのプレートを組み合わせたシステムで、機能、視覚的な面でシンプルで手に取りやすい。また、フィッティングルームも同じ素材を使い、ドアは片開き式の1枚プレートでグレーに彩色してあり、背後の壁に打ち付けたメタルのプレートとデザイン的な調和を見せる。固定客も多く、ミニサロンは街で踊り疲れた人のための格好の場である。

Moudjahidin is a hip-hop fashion boutique, with an Arab-style interior, located on the bustling tourism and shopping street Le Halles. Through the entrance one finds a cash register and a men's sales floor. In the center of the boutique is a minisalon, a shoe section and fitting rooms. In the back is the ladies' sales floor. There is plenty of space to dance to the music. Mirrors and mosquelike decorations are placed throughout the shop to enhance the mood.

The shoes display uses a combination of water pipe and aluminum plates to achieve a visually and functionally simple system. The fitting rooms use the same materials. Each has a single-aluminum-plate swinging door painted gray, behind which is a metal plate that has been nailed to the wall. Together, they achieve a harmony of design.

The minisalon is a place for people who are tired from dancing in nearby clubs to sit down in chairs have a rest. It has many regular patrons.

店内中央にあるミニサロン　Minisalon

Left.　ダンスフロアとしても利用されているレジ前のスペース　Cashier
Center.　アルミパンチングメタルと水道管で構成されたシューズディスプレイ　Shoes display
Right.　「アラブ」をテーマにまとめられた店内　Space in front of the cashier

§ MOUDJAHIDIN DATA §
Address: 17 Piere Lescot Reriers Paris France　Phone: 01-42331490
Opening date: March 2001　Building Area: 90m²
Business hours: 10:00〜22:00

店内奥のコーナー　Corner of the shop

GALERIE FÜR SCHMUCK
Fashion shop/Berlin

小物やアクセサリー類の展示には、商品自体のデザインやカラー等を引き立たせる空間の雰囲気づくりが大事な要素となる。このGALERIE FÜR SCHMUCKはAnna Schetelich氏が経営するショールームで、ベルリンを中心にドイツ全域から若手新進デザイナーのアイデアに満ちた商品を集め展示販売している。

45㎡ある店内には、カラーのアクリルボードが天井から吊り下げられ、床からは複数の糸で押さえ商品を陳列している。また、天井と壁に取り付けられたライトをスポット的にボードに当て、その不規則な反射光が天井や壁の上で宝石のような光の像になる。同じボードに2つの光線が入れば、ダイヤのような立体感も得られる。

アクリルボードは軽いため、1本の糸で吊り下げられると微妙に動くことは自然の成り行きである。その度に乱れた光が空間に舞う。これはMarkus Böttcher氏とオーナーのアイデアで、Burthart Ellinghaus氏の製作によるものである。

To display small articles and accessories, the designer of Galerie Für Schmuck created an atmosphere that emphasizes the designs and colors of the merchandise itself. This showroom, managed by Anna Schetelich, deals in creative merchandise from young, up-and-coming designers from throughout Germany, but primarily Berlin.

In the 45-square-meters interior, pieces of colored acrylic board are hung from the ceiling, and merchandise on display is held in place by threads attached to the floor. Spotlights are aimed at the boards, which reflect the light irregularly to cast jewel-like images back on the ceiling and walls. If two beams of light hit a single board, the result is a diamondlike three-dimensionality.

The lightweight acrylic boards, each held up by a single thread, naturally move, causing light to dance throughout the gallery. This mechanism was conceived by the owner and Markus Böttcher and realized by Burthart Ellinghaus.

糸で支えられたディスプレイテーブル　Detail of the displaytable

ディスプレイテーブルに反射した光は壁や天井で不思議な光の像を結ぶ　Displaytable

ファサード　Facade

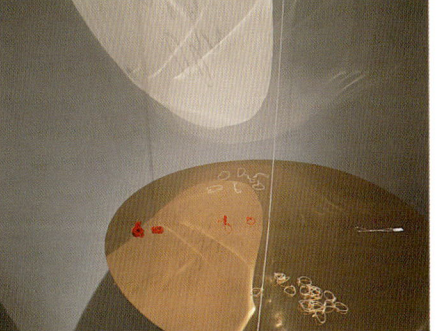

店内全景　A whole view of the shop

ディスプレイテーブル　Displaytable

§ GALERIE FÜR SCHMUCK DATA §
Address: Auguststrasse 26 10117 Berlin Germany　Phone: 030-28045905
Interior designer: Anna Schetelich+Markus Böttcher
Opening date: 21th. October 2000
Building Area: 45m^2　Business hours: 14:00~19:00 (Tue.~Fri.)　13:00~18:00 (Sat.)

マンゴカラーのセラミックで構成されたディスプレイコーナー　A view of the shop

ファサード　Facade

ニューコレクションのコーナー　A view of the shop

MANGO
Boutique/London

コベントガーデンにあるニールストリートは小さな店舗が軒を連ねており、ロンドンらしさを残す魅力的な通りのひとつである。MANGOは世界の主要都市に出店し、日本でも数店フランチャイズ展開をしており、バルセロナに本部がある。

マンゴカラーのガラス張りのファサードと黒のロゴマーク、エントランスまわりの吹き抜け空間のカラーコントラストには、グラフィカルな力強さが感じられる。店内はレジカウンターのあるフロアをベースに、半階上下にスキップさせた3層構成で、入り口から各フロアへの視覚的アプローチを可能にしている。上下階の中央にはセラミックプレートを配したショーケースがある。オレンジ色のレジデンス風で、スペインを連想させる。木を使用したディスプレイ什器を随所に置き、光を内蔵したボックスをディスプレイ台として使用するなど、商品のイメージアップにさまざまな試みがなされている。

Shop-lined Neal Street in Covent Garden is one of several streets that retains the charm of London. Mango has an outlet on Neal Street and others in major cities throughout the world; it has several franchises in Japan and its headquarters are in Barcelona.

There is a tangible, graphic boldness to the mango-colored glass windows of the facade, the black logo and the contrasting colors in the well surrounding the entrance. The level that includes the entrance and the cash-register counter has a level above it and another below it. All three are visible from the entrance. A showcase for ceramic plates is found in the center of both the top level and the bottom level. The orange-colored interior brings to mind Spain.

Furniture for displaying merchandise is found throughout Mango, and the designers have used a number of contrivances, such as an internally lighted box stand, to display their wares favorably.

§ MANGO DATA §
Address: 8-12 Neal Street London WC2 UK   Phone: 020-74343179
Interior designer: Damian Sanchez   Building Area: 750m²
Business hours: 10:00~19:00 (Mon. Tue. Wed.)   10:00~20:00 (Thu.)   12:00~18:00 (Sun.)

吹き抜けのエントランス空間　Entrance

ファサード　Facade

COMPTOIR GASCON
Food shop/London

ディスプレイの様子　Display

メーンカウンター　Main counter

ロンドンの中央食品市場、セントラルマーケットに隣接するこの店舗は、フランス南西部の農業地帯の食品を販売するデリカショップである。近年、特にイギリス人のグルメへの関心は高まりを見せているが、フランス料理とその食材は人気の的となっている。

デパートと違って売り場がセクション化されていないため、専門店では商品の配置やディスプレイが店全体の雰囲気を左右することになる。ここでは中央に新鮮な野菜、果物を丸太を台にして置き、チーズやケーキ、オードブル用の食品をメーンカウンターに納めている。一方の壁面にはショッピングバッグとワインコーナー、フレンチスタイルのテーブル用品をサンプルにして、フランス南西部の牧歌的な写真をバックに陳列。ファサードにはパン類を並べて外から見えるようにして、ジャムや果汁等のビン類は外光を受けてカラフルな光を放っている。職人、店のスタッフはすべてイギリス人である。

This delicatessen neighboring Central Market, London's primary food marketplace, sells foods from the agricultural area of southwest France. Its French food and ingredients have garnered increasing appreciation in recent years, particularly from English gourmands.

Specialty stores are not divided into sections like department stores, and product placement affects the overall atmosphere. At Comptoir Gascon, fresh vegetables and fruits are found on a central stand made from logs. Cheese, cakes and hors d'oeuvre ingredients are kept on the main counter. A shopping bag and wine section, along with samples of French-style tableware, is placed near one wall, on which pastoral photographs of southwest France have been arranged.

Breads have been placed at the front of the store so that they can be seen from outside. Exterior light filters colorfully through jars of jam and bottles of juice. The entire staff of Comptoir Gascon is English.

§ COMPTOIR GASCON DATA §

Address: 61-63 Charterhouse Street London EC1 UK   Phone :020-76080851
Opening date: 13th. February 2001   Building Area: 240m²
Business hours: 8:00~20:00 (Mon.~Fri.)   8:00~18:00 (Sat.)

ファサード　Facade

光るディスプレイ台　Display space

高さ2.5メートルの女性のパンツ像　Mannequin

JITROIS
Boutique/London

レザーファッションで人気がある、パリのJEAN CLAUDE JITROISのロンドン店で、スローンストリートにある。界隈はミラノやパリのファッションブランドの、ロンドン1の激戦区といってもよい地域で、ミレニアムを期に改装した店も数多い。

店内中央には高さ2.5mの、黒いパンツをまとった女性の腰から下の立像が立ちはだかり、インパクトのある空間演出がなされている。その背後には、ロン・アラッドのメタリックのソファが2つ置かれている。店内の空白となっているスペースには、市販のメタルのチェーンをドレープのようにして吊り下げ、ハンガー什器のメタルと商品のレザーとフィットさせている。フィッティングルームはカラーのモザイクタイルで、空間に華やかさを添えている。

The London store of Jean Claude Jitrois, Paris' popular leather fashion brand, is located on Sloane Street. The neighborhood is the number one battleground in London for Milano and Paris fashion brands. A number of the retailers there remodeled on the occasion of the millenium.

In the center of the shop stands a 2.5-meter statue of a woman's lower body clad in black pants, lending impact to the space and blocking the way. Behind it are two Ron Alad metallic sofas. In the vacant interior of the store are draped metal chains, which are for sale; these fit in well with the metal of the hangers and the leather of the clothing. The color mosaic tiles in the fitting rooms add a gaiety to the space.

§ JITROIS DATA §
Address: 6F Sloane Street London SW1 UK　Phone: 020-72456300
Interior designer: Jean Claude Jitrois
Opening date: January 1999　Building Area 185m²
Business hours: 10:00~19:00 (Mon.~Fri.)　11:00~18:00 (Sat.)

BOTTENHEIM
Fashion shop/Berlin

ジーンズで神格化されたLevi Strausは、ドイツ・ブッテンハイムの生まれで、彼の出身地名にちなんで始められたのがこのショップ兼ショールームである。店内がアパートのようなので、俗に「アパートメント」と呼ばれている。マネジャーのKonstantin氏は、「ファッションデザイナーやミュージシャンを目指す若者のタレント性を見いだし、ビジネスとしての登竜門となれば」とその熱意を語る。商品はヨーロッパ全域から取り寄せ、月1回くらいのローテーションで展示物を変えているという。また、このアパートメントではミュージシャンのCD開発にも力を入れており、発表会やパーティーを催してコミュニケーションの場を提供しその期待も大きい。

Bottenheim is a shop and showroom associated with the Bottenheim, Germany, birthplace of blue jeans deity Levi Straus. The interior of the shop looks like an apartment and has been nicknamed "the apartment." Mr. Konstantin, the manager, speaks zealously of the shop as a scouting ground for talented young people who want to be fashion designers or musicians, and a possible gateway into those businesses for them. The merchandise was gathered from throughout Europe, and display items are rotated on a monthly basis. Moreover, the apartment produces musicians' CDs. It hosts news conferences and parties and is well known as a communication hub.

§ BOTTENHEIM DATA §

Address: Neue Schönhauser Str. 15 10178 Berlin Germany   Phone: 030-27594460
Interior designer: Konstantin
Opening date: March 2000   Building Area: 80m²
Business hours: 12:00~20:00 (Mon.~Fri.)   12:00~16:00 (Sat.)

寝室風のディスプレイ   Display

1st.   店内全景   A whole view of the shop
2nd.   歴史を記した文章とともに飾られたビンテージジーンズ   Display

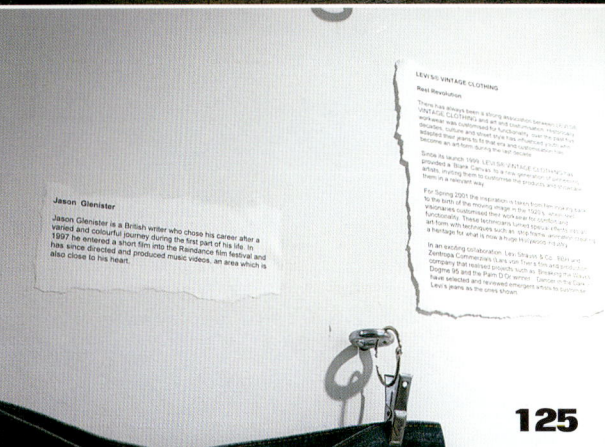

ライブラリー。ソファでくつろぎながら商品を買い求めることができる　Library　　　隣接するトレーニングジムからのアプローチ　Drink bar

階段　Staircase

FRESH&WILD
Health food shop/London

Organic FoodsとNatural Remedies、これは有機食品、自然療法と訳したらよいのだろうか。ロンドンに限らず世界的な傾向として、健康食品に対する関心は高まるばかりである。FRESH&WILDは会社創設以来6年めで、現在ロンドンを中心に6店舗があり、このSoho店は最新のもので、ピカデリー・サーカスから歩いて3分くらいのところにある。

開店と同時に隣のビルも改築され、テナントとして入居したトレーニングジムのレセプションと結ばれ、トレーニングを終えた人たちがジュースを飲んだり、買い物をしていくなど健康的にアクセスしている。1階はレジを中心に各種のミネラルウオーター、無農薬野菜、果物、テイクアウト用の食材、パンコーナーなどがある。2階は健康、自然薬品のコーナーで、棚には世界各国から集められた数多くのサンプルが並び、データを公表している。窓辺にはライブラリーもあり、ソファでくつろぎながら商品を買い求めることができる。小さい店ではあるが、リフトがあるなど、優しさのある店舗設計といえる。

The movement toward natural remedies and organic and health foods continues to grow not only in London, but throughout the world. Now in its sixth year, the company Fresh & Wild has six stores, centered in London. The Soho outlet, which is the newest, is a three-minute walk from Piccadilly Circus.

When the store opened, the building next door was altered and a training gym moved in. Fresh & Wild and the gym decided to share a reception area. Gym clients who have finished their workouts go to Fresh & Wild to drink juice, shop and otherwise take advantage of the health-oriented store.

The first floor contains a central cash register, various mineral waters, organic fruits and vegetables, takeout foods and a bread section. The second floor is the health and natural remedies section. Its shelves contain samples gathered from around the world and are labeled with information about them. By the windows are a library and a sofa where shoppers can relax.

This Fresh & Wild outlet, though small, features a warm design that includes an elevator.

§ FRESH&WILD DATA §

Address: 69-75 Brewer Street London W1 UK　Phone: 020-74343179
Architect: Richard Hywel Evans
Opening date: 16th. December 2000　Building Area: 280m²
Business hours: 7:30~22:30 (Mon.~Sat.)　11:30~20:30 (Sun.)

CHRISTA RENIERS
Jewelry store/Brussels

ブリュッセルの証券取引所近くのR.A. Dansaert通り周辺は、再開発の真っただ中にあり、EUの首都として徐々にではあるが街並みがリフレッシュされ、飲食店等が急増している。このCHRISTA RENIERSは、この10年のうちにヘアーサロンからバーになり、そしてこの店になった。

インテリアは宝石店特有の閉鎖的な雰囲気を感じさせないデザインとなっている。シンプルにテーブルを配し、合板のディスプレイ台を壁面に配列。その奥はアトリエで、トップライトから降り注ぐ光はゲートのようなアプローチと相まって、建築的な美しさが感じられる。入り口にある唯一のディスプレイは、全面ガラスのショーウインドーより興味をそそる心理効果がありそうである。

この店のオーナーでありジュエリーデザイナーでもあるReniers氏は、デザイン歴10年。他にGent市にも店舗を持っており、年間10,000ピースのジュエリーを売り上げているとのこと。全人口が1,000万人のベルギーであるから、かなりの売れっ子といえる。

The area around R.A. Dansaert street, near Brussels' stock exchange, is in the middle of redevelopment, and the look of the stores and houses on the streets of this European Union capital is gradually being refreshed, with eating and drinking establishments rapidly multiplying. Christa Reniers transformed itself from a hair salon into a bar over the course of 10 years before becoming the shop it is today.

The interior design avoids creating the closed atmosphere peculiar to jewelry stores. Tables are arranged simply and veneer-board display stands are arrayed against the wall. Beyond the tables and display stands is an atelier, where light pouring down from the skylight combines with the gatelike approach to impart a sense of architectural beauty. The single display in the entrance seems to create a more compelling psychological effect than would an all-glass show window.

A jewelry designer with 10 years' experience named Reniers owns this shop. He also owns a shop in the city of Gent, and sells 10,000 pieces of jewelry per year. Considering that the population of Belgium is only 10 million, Mr. Reniers is quite a hit.

§ CHRISTA RENIERS DATA §

Address: Rue Antoine Dansaert Straat 29. 1000 Brussels Belgium   Phone: 02-5144615
Architect: Frank de Grove
Opening date: August 1999   Building Area: 80m²
Business hours: 10:00~18:00 (Mon.~Sat.)   Regular Holiday: Sunday

ショップからアトリエへのアプローチ　Passage

店内全景　A whole view of the shop

ディスプレイ　Display

ウインドーディスプレイ　Showwindow